CBMCS
Multicultural Training Program
Program
Participant Workbook

CBMCS
Multicultural Training Program
Participant Workbook

Aghop Der-Karabetian
University of La Verne
Richard H. Dana
Regional Research Institute for Human Services, Portland State University
Glenn C. Gamst
University of La Verne

SAGE Publications

Los Angeles • London • New Delhi • Singapore

For information:

SAGE Publications, Inc.
2455 Teller Road
Thousand Oaks, California 91320
E-mail: order@sagepub.com

SAGE Publications Ltd.
1 Oliver's Yard
55 City Road
London EC1Y 1SP
United Kingdom

SAGE Publications India Pvt. Ltd.
B 1/I 1 Mohan Cooperative Industrial Area
Mathura Road, New Delhi 110 044
India

SAGE Publications Asia-Pacific Pte. Ltd.
33 Pekin Street #02-01
Far East Square
Singapore 048763

Printed in the United States of America

Library of Congress Cataloging-in-Publication Data

Der-Karabetian, Aghop.
CBMCS multicultural training program: Participant workbook/Aghop Der-Karabetian, Richard H. Dana, Glenn C. Gamst.
    p. cm.
Includes bibliographical references.
ISBN 978-1-4129-5945-2 (pbk.)
    1. Cross-cultural counseling—United States. 2. Social work with minorities—United States. 3. Multiculturalism—United States. I. Dana, Richard H. (Richard Henry), 1927- II. Gamst, Glenn. III. Title.

BF636.7.C76D47 2008
158'.3—dc22   2007049539

Printed on acid-free paper.

08   09   10   11   12   10   9   8   7   6   5   4   3   2   1

Acquiring Editor:	Kassie Graves
Editorial Assistant:	Veronica Novak
Production Editor:	Sarah K. Quesenberry
Copy Editor:	Linda Gray
Typesetter:	C&M Digitals (P) Ltd.
Proofreader:	Jenifer Kooiman
Cover Designer:	Ravi Balasuriya
Marketing Manager:	Carmel Schrire

Contents

Introduction

Welcome to the CBMCS Multicultural Training Program! The purpose of this workbook is to provide resources that will facilitate and enhance your participation in the training program.

A Brief Background

As a mental health services provider, you are in the front lines of responding to the surgeon general's (U.S. Department of Health and Human Services, 2001) call to deliver multiculturally competent care. The surgeon general's report

> documents the existence of striking disparities for minorities in mental health services and the underlying knowledge base. Racial and ethnic minorities have less access to mental health services than do whites. They are less likely to receive needed care. When they receive care, it is more likely to be poor in quality.
>
> . . . A major finding . . . is that racial and ethnic minorities bear a greater burden from unmet mental health needs and thus suffer a greater loss to their overall health and productivity. (p. 3)

The reasons for failure of training resources to benefit ethnic minority clients is not entirely understood, but it may be due to reluctance of some service providers to discuss racial/cultural issues as germane to treatment regardless of their own ethnic background (Maxie, Arnold, & Stephenson, 2006; Tatum, 2002). Therefore, it is important to accelerate the learning process by integrating experiential and personalized training modalities. Combining cognitive and affective training modalities facilitates the process of incorporating competency training into professional skills. Such interpersonal skills training for professionals encourages their client populations to internalize identity perspectives diverging markedly from the personal constructions and interpretations characterizing most middle-class European American providers. These identity perspectives can potentially foster personal growth, wholeness, and well-being in clients and increase their feelings of being accepted and understood in cross-racial/cross-ethnic mental health service delivery.

Our original goal was to develop a brief (or short-form) self-report multicultural competence scale that could be easily administered and scored and routinely used to empirically ascertain community mental health practitioners' multicultural training needs (i.e., staff self-perceived cultural competence). A summary of this work can be found in a report titled "Cultural Competency Revised: The California Brief Multicultural Competence Scale (Gamst et al., 2004). Over time, this goal was revised and expanded to include the development of a training manual/curriculum for each of the four subscales identified in the CBMCS. The four modules in this training program correspond to the four subscales identified in the measure—namely, Multicultural Knowledge, Awareness of Cultural Barriers, Sensitivity and Responsiveness to Consumers, and Sociocultural Diversities. The fourth subscale (and the module) explicitly addresses the following multiple identities: socioeconomic status, disability, older adults, lesbians/gay men, and heterosexual women/men.

During the CBMCS Multicultural Training Program, participants may experience parts of the training program from the perspective of the following developmental stages (Bennett, 1986; Hammer, Bennett, & Wiseman, 2003):

Stage 1: Disinterest/denial of differences

Stage 2: Defense against differences; unique viability of own culture

Stage 3: Differences minimized, masked by institutional privilege

Stage 4: Acceptance of cultural differences/worldviews

Stage 5: Adaptation to differences in perception, behaviors, thinking

Stage 6: Integration—self-perception eases movement between cultures

Beginning with denial (Stage 1), the stages proceed through defense (Stage 2) to minimization of differences (Stage 3), in which differences are merely acknowledged and tolerated without being accepted. Acceptance (Stage 4) implies that the cultural perspectives responsible for differences are comprehensible and acceptable. Middle-class European American professionals need training or a history of atypical life experiences to arrive at this stage. A variety of specific cultural awareness training approaches to achieve Stage 4 competence have been available for many years, although many of these techniques are rarely applied with professional psychologists. Adaptation in Stage 5 requires a temporary modification of thought and behavior in the presence of culturally different behaviors. American Peace Corps volunteers who learn to think and behave appropriately in situ provide a Stage 5 illustration in which worldview modifications become habitual, permitting the culturally appropriate actions of bicultural or multicultural individuals (LaFromboise, Coleman, & Gerton, 1993). Integration (Stage 6) implies contextual relativism, a more generalized ability to evaluate phenomena relative to a cultural context and the essence of ethnorelativistic thinking.

The CBMCS Multicultural Training Program is designed to be applicable across mental health settings and providers with different professional backgrounds and affiliations. This training program will continue to evolve, based in part on feedback received from program participants and ongoing program evaluation efforts. Findings from outcome research will evaluate the effectiveness of the training process and the utility of an empirically derived training model. The CBMCS Multicultural Training Program should contribute to improving the quality of mental health services for all consumers.

Use of This Workbook

This Participant Workbook is intended as a companion resource for the CBMCS Multicultural Training Program. It includes the following components:

1. *PowerPoint slides:* Copies of the PowerPoint slides used by the trainers are provided to avoid distractions due to taking notes during the presentation. However, space is provided next to each slide for reflections and questions you may have to share during or after the training.

2. *Module handouts and activities:* During the training you will be asked to use various handouts and participate in small-group activities. Having these handouts and directions for activities easily accessible will save time and make them available for future reference.

3. *Participant module evaluation forms:* These forms are provided for you to give feedback about the training program and the way you experience it. The training program will continue to evolve based on the feedback received from you. There is a separate form for each module. As trainers may instruct you, it will be best if you complete the forms at the end of each training module and return them to the trainers. To preserve anonymity, please do not put your name on the evaluation forms. Your comments and suggestions are very important.

4. *The CBMCS Self-Report Measure of Multicultural Competence:* The CBMCS measure is composed of 21 items to assess the four self-reported areas of multicultural competence (mentioned above). Trainers or your organization may instruct you to complete it at the beginning of the training or some time before the training. Or they may ask you to complete it before as well as at the end of the training to gauge the changes that might have occurred. Whether or not you put your name on the measure depends on your agency or organization. There is a demographic questionnaire attached to the CBMCS measure primarily for research purposes. A transformation table is also provided to transform raw scores to percentile score.

References

Bennett, M. J. (1986). A developmental approach to training for intercultural sensitivity. *International Journal of Intercultural Relations, 10,* 179–196.

Gamst, G., Dana, R. H., Der-Karabetian, A., Aragon, M., Arellano, L., Morrow, G., & Martenson, L. (2004). Cultural competency revised: The California Brief Multicultural Competence Scale. *Measurement and Evaluation in Counseling and Development, 37,* 163–187.

Hammer, M. R., Bennett, M. J., & Wiseman, R. (2003). Measuring intercultural sensitivity: The Intercultural Development Inventory. *International Journal of Intercultural Relations, 27,* 421–443.

LaFromboise, T., Coleman, H. L. K., & Gerton, J. (1993). Psychological impact of biculturalism: Evidence and theory. *Psychological Bulletin, 114,* 395–412.

Maxie, A. C., Arnold, D. H., & Stephenson, M. (2006). Do therapists address ethnic and racial differences in cross-cultural psychotherapy? *Psychotherapy: Theory, Research, Practice, Training,* 85–98.

Tatum, B. (2002). Breaking the silence. In P. S. Rothenberg (Ed.), *White privilege: Essential readings on the other side of racism* (pp. 115–120). New York: Worth.

U.S. Department of Health and Human Services. (2001). *Mental health: Culture, race, and ethnicity: A supplement to mental health: A report of the surgeon general—Executive summary.* Rockville, MD: Author.

1

RAL
OGE

Call
Dawn v. SAU

Slides

**Module 1
Multicultural Knowledge**

1

Acknowledgments

2

Richard H. Dana, Regional Research Institute for
Human Services, Portland State University
Glenn C. Gamst, University of La Verne
Aghop Der-Karabetian, University of La Verne

With Contributions From
Leticia Arellano-Morales, University of La Verne
Marya Endriga, California State University, Sacramento
Robbin Huff-Musgrove, San Bernardino County Department of
Behavioral Health
Gloria Morrow, Private Practice

With Generous Support From
California Department of Mental Health–Office of
Multicultural Services
Eli Lilly Foundation
California Mental Health Directors Association
California Institute of Mental Health
University of La Verne, La Verne, CA

Introductions

3

Module 1 Overview

1. CBMCS Development
2. Cultural Competency Defined
3. Historic and Contemporary Overview of the Four Major Ethnic Groups in the U.S.
4. Health Disparities
5. Recognizing Deficiencies in Research Conducted on Minorities
6. Psychosocial Factors to Consider When Providing Services to a Culturally Diverse Consumer Population
7. Providing Culturally Competent Mental Health Assessment and Diagnosis
8. Understanding and Evaluating Wellness, Recovery, and Resiliency

---

The California Brief Multicultural Competence Scale and Training Program

- This scale consists of 4 subscales:
  - Multicultural Knowledge
  - Awareness of Cultural Barriers
  - Sensitivity and Responsiveness to Consumers
  - Sociocultural Diversities
- An 8-hour training program is available for each subscale.
- The CBMCS is a 21-item self-assessment of cultural competence.

(Gamst et al., 2004)

Purpose of Module 1

- This training focuses on the four racial/ethnic/cultural groups that have experienced the greatest levels of historical oppression in the U.S.; however, this training allows for inclusion of other racial/ethnic/cultural groups and communities.
- Today the surgeon general reports that these same groups continue to experience disparities in access to, quality of, and outcomes of mental health care.

Setting the Tone

- This process may generate strong emotions
- Need to set and agree to ground rules
  - Respect
  - Confidentiality
  - Active listening
  - Nonjudgmental comments
  - Group input
  - Address comments to trainer/facilitator

CBMCS

Goals and Objectives

- To obtain historic, contemporary, and demographic information on the four main ethnic/racial/cultural groups in the U.S.
- To examine sources of bias that have resulted in inadequate services and curtailed use of services available to these groups
- To become aware of empirical knowledge concerning the mental health status of ethnic, racial, cultural groups
- To recognize deficiencies in related research
- To explore implications for practice

CBMCS

Defining Some Terms

- Race
- Ethnicity
- Culture
- Etic
- Emic
- Collectivism
- Individualism
- Colonialism

CBMCS

Transitional Stages of Change

- Denial (of differences)
- Defense (against differences)
- Minimization of differences (bury differences under cultural similarities)
- Acceptance (of cultural differences)
- Adaptation (of behavior and thinking to that difference)

(Bennett, 1986; Hammer, Bennett, & Wiseman, 2003)

Definition of Cultural Competence

- Individual Cultural Competence: "The state of being capable of functioning effectively in the context of cultural differences."

- Organizational Cultural Competence: A set of congruent behaviors, attitudes, and policies that come together in a system, agency, or among professionals and enable that system, agency, or those professionals to work effectively in cross-cultural situations.

- Culturally Competent Mental Health Care: Will rely on historical experiences of prejudice, discrimination, racism and other culture-specific beliefs about health or illness, culturally unique symptoms and interventions with each cultural group to inform treatment.

(Cross, Bazron, Dennis, & Isaacs, 1989; Pope-Davis, Coleman, Liu, & Toporek, 2003)

Organizational Levels of Cultural Competence

- Consumer
- Practitioner
- Administration and senior management
- Policy

(Cross, Bazron, Dennis, & Isaacs, 1989; Isaacs & Benjamin, 1991)

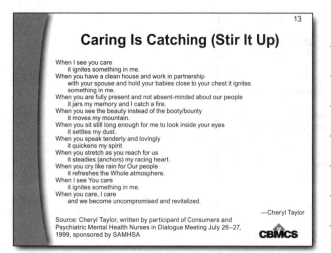

Caring Is Catching (Stir It Up)

When I see you care
    it ignites something in me.
When you have a clean house and work in partnership
    with your spouse and hold your babies close to your chest it ignites
    something in me.
When you are fully present and not absent-minded about our people
    it jars my memory and I catch a fire.
When you see the beauty instead of the booty/bounty
    it moves my mountain.
When you sit still long enough for me to look inside your eyes
    it settles my dust.
When you speak tenderly and lovingly
    it quickens my spirit
When you stretch as you reach for us
    it steadies (anchors) my racing heart.
When you cry like rain for Our people
    it refreshes the Whole atmosphere.
When I see You care
    it ignites something in me.
When you care, I care
    and we become uncompromised and revitalized.

—Cheryl Taylor

Source: Cheryl Taylor, written by participant of Consumers and
Psychiatric Mental Health Nurses in Dialogue Meeting July 26–27,
1999, sponsored by SAMHSA

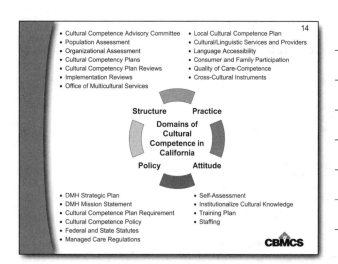

- Cultural Competence Advisory Committee
- Population Assessment
- Organizational Assessment
- Cultural Competency Plans
- Cultural Competency Plan Reviews
- Implementation Reviews
- Office of Multicultural Services

- Local Cultural Competence Plan
- Cultural/Linguistic Services and Providers
- Language Accessibility
- Consumer and Family Participation
- Quality of Care-Competence
- Cross-Cultural Instruments

Structure   **Practice**

Domains of Cultural Competence in California

Policy   **Attitude**

- DMH Strategic Plan
- DMH Mission Statement
- Cultural Competence Plan Requirement
- Cultural Competence Policy
- Federal and State Statutes
- Managed Care Regulations

- Self-Assessment
- Institutionalize Cultural Knowledge
- Training Plan
- Staffing

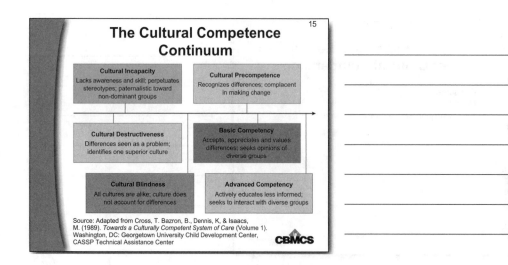

The Cultural Competence Continuum

Cultural Incapacity
Lacks awareness and skill; perpetuates stereotypes; paternalistic toward non-dominant groups

Cultural Precompetence
Recognizes differences; complacent in making change

Cultural Destructiveness
Differences seen as a problem; identifies one superior culture

Basic Competency
Accepts, appreciates and values differences; seeks opinions of diverse groups

Cultural Blindness
All cultures are alike; culture does not account for differences

Advanced Competency
Actively educates less informed; seeks to interact with diverse groups

Source: Adapted from Cross, T. Bazron, B., Dennis, K, & Isaacs,
M. (1989). *Towards a Culturally Competent System of Care* (Volume 1).
Washington, DC: Georgetown University Child Development Center,
CASSP Technical Assistance Center

The Five Essential Elements of Cultural Competence

Organizational	Individual
• Valuing Diversity	• Awareness and Acceptance of Difference
• Cultural Self-Assessment	
• Managing for the Dynamics of Difference	• Awareness of Own Cultural Values
• Institutionalization of Cultural Knowledge	• Understanding Dynamics of Difference
• Adaptation to Diversity Policies, Structure, Values, Services	• Development of Cultural Knowledge
	• Ability to Adapt Practice to the Cultural Context of Client

(Cross, Bazron, Dennis, & Isaacs, 1989; Isaacs & Benjamin, 1991; see also Arredondo & Arciniega, 2001, for strategies and techniques)

Activity: Dialogue on Cultural Competence

- Select a recorder and a reporter.
- Brainstorm one-word descriptors of what cultural competence means to you.
- Take these descriptors and develop a definition of cultural competence.
- Reporters will share your group's definition.

The Need for Cultural Competence

- To ensure that appropriate assessment, diagnosis, and treatment are provided to culturally diverse communities
- To increase utilization rates when mental health services are necessary
- To improve the overall quality of services and outcomes
- To respond to current California demographics

(See Constantine & Sue, 2005, for more details on the APA guidelines)

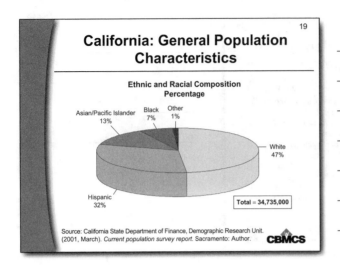

California: General Population Characteristics

Ethnic and Racial Composition Percentage

Asian/Pacific Islander 13%
Black 7%
Other 1%
White 47%
Hispanic 32%

Total = 34,735,000

Source: California State Department of Finance, Demographic Research Unit. (2001, March). *Current population survey report.* Sacramento: Author.

CBMCS

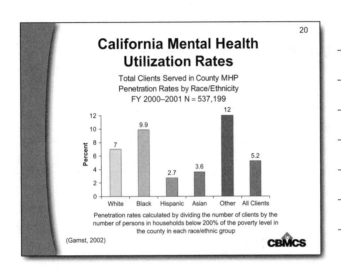

California Mental Health Utilization Rates

Total Clients Served in County MHP
Penetration Rates by Race/Ethnicity
FY 2000–2001 N = 537,199

White 7
Black 9.9
Hispanic 2.7
Asian 3.6
Other 12
All Clients 5.2

Penetration rates calculated by dividing the number of clients by the number of persons in households below 200% of the poverty level in the county in each race/ethnic group

(Gamst, 2002)

CBMCS

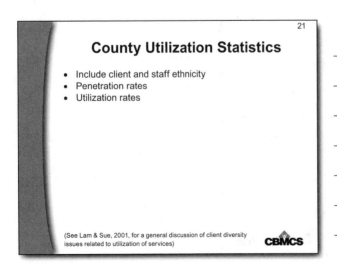

County Utilization Statistics

- Include client and staff ethnicity
- Penetration rates
- Utilization rates

(See Lam & Sue, 2001, for a general discussion of client diversity issues related to utilization of services)

CBMCS

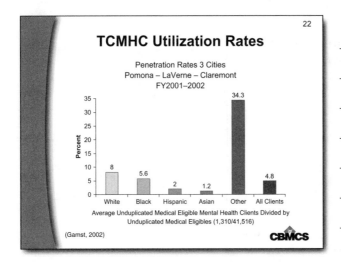

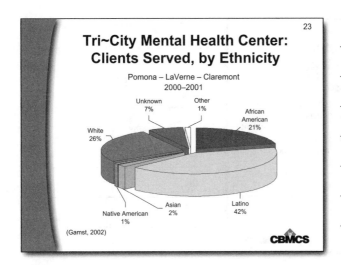

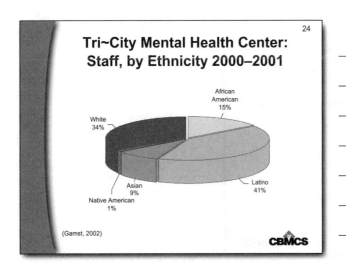

Historic and Contemporary Overview

- Four Ethnic/Racial Groups in the U.S.:
  - African American
  - Latino American
  - Asian American
  - Native American Indian
- History
- Demographics
- Mental Health Status

CBMCS

The Impact of Oppression on Communities

Tools

- Unjust use of power
- Assumption of superiority
- Racism
- Sexism
- Ageism
- Classism
- Dehumanization

Consequences

- Marginalization/ discrimination
- Limited economic mobility (poverty)
- Limited educational mobility
- Interference with access to resources
- Disparities in health care

(Feagin & Feagin, 1999)

CBMCS

Activity: Tools and Consequences of Oppression

- Break into small groups.
- In what ways have you experienced and/or perpetrated the tools of oppression?
- What are the consequences of oppression you have experienced or witnessed?
- Group reports back.

CBMCS

History of Oppression in the U.S.: African Americans

- African Americans:
  - Legacy of slavery
  - Racism and discrimination
  - Race and science
    - Mental Health Service Deficits
    - Racial differences
    - Racial designations
    - Eugenics and euthenics
    - IQ testing/mental retardation
    - Sterilization laws
    - Tuskegee (syphilis experiment)
  - Mental health "cool out"

(Christian, 1999; Dana, 2002b; Guthrie, 1976)

History of Oppression in the U.S.: American Indians/Alaskan Natives

- American Indians/Alaskan Natives:
  - Land confiscation and displacement
  - Broken treaties
  - Slavery and religious conversion
  - Genocide
  - Annihilation of cultural and spiritual beliefs
  - Boarding school, forced assimilation
  - Missionary movement

(Choney, Berryhill-Paapke, & Robbins, 1995)

History of Oppression in the U.S.: Asian Americans/Pacific Islanders

- Asian Americans/Pacific Islanders:
  - Taxation and economic hardship
    - Japanese Exclusion Bill of 1924
    - Concentration (internment) camps
    - Magnuson Act
    - Labor exploitation (forced labor for Chinese)
    - Chinese Exclusion Act of 1882
  - Immigration/refugee

(Locke, 1998)

History of Oppression in the U.S.: Hispanics/Latino/a Americans

31

- Hispanics/Latino Americans:
  - Wars
    - War for Texas independence 1835
    - Mexican War of 1846–1848
  - Treaty of Guadalupe Hidalgo
  - American occupation
    - Loss of land and natural resources
  - Immigration
    - 1912–1920 campesinos
    - 1924 immigration law
    - Bracero Program 1939–1945
  - Mid-20th century
    - Sleepy Lagoon Incident 1942
    - Zoot Suit Riots 1942

(Locke, 1998; Microsoft Encarta Online Encyclopedia, 1998)

Clinical Implications of Oppression *(DSM-IV/DSM-IV-TR)*

32

- Depression
- PTSD
- Racial trauma as diagnostic category
- Transgenerational trauma
- Suicide
- Substance abuse
- Misdiagnosis
- Physical illness
- Pathology/nonpathology (mental health/behavioral health)***

(Dana, 2007)

Challenges to the Mental Health System: U.S. Surgeon General's Report

33

- U.S. mental health system may be ill prepared to meet the mental health needs of racial/ethnic groups due to deficiencies in level of cultural competence among service providers of all types (e.g., psychiatrists, therapists, case managers).
- Unique cultural differences exist among racial/ethnic groups with regard to coping styles, utilization of services, help-seeking attitudes and behaviors, and the use of family and community as resources.

(U.S. Department of Health and Human Services, 2001)

Areas of Service Concern: U.S. Surgeon General's Report

34

- Need
- Availability
- Accessibility
- Utilization
- Appropriateness
- Outcomes

Health Disparities: African Americans

35

- African Americans:
  - May be at higher risk of mental disorders than whites due to socioeconomic differences (Reiger et al., 1993)
  - Tend to be underrepresented in outpatient treatment, overrepresented (by twice as many) in inpatient treatment (Snowden, 2001; Snowden & Cheung, 1990), with difficult access to culturally competent services (Snowden & Yamada, 2005)
  - More likely to use the emergency room for mental health problems than whites (Snowden, 2001)
  - Higher rates of misdiagnosis compared with whites and, consequently, mistakes that lead to the use of inappropriate medications

(U.S. Department of Health and Human Services, 2001)

Health Disparities: American Indians/Alaskan Natives

36

- American Indians/Alaskan Natives:
  - Few epidemiological surveys of mental health and mental disorders
  - Depression a significant problem for many American Indians/Alaskan Indians
  - Higher risk of alcohol abuse and dependence
  - High rates of suicide
  - U.S. veterans, higher prevalence rates of PTSD than whites

(U.S. Department of Health and Human Services, 2001)

Health Disparities: Asian Americans/Pacific Islanders

37

- Asian Americans/Pacific Islanders:
  - Model minority myth and other subgroup stereotypes
  - Underutilization due to stigma and shame: Delay seeking services until problems become very serious
  - Access barriers due to lack of language proficiency of service providers

(U.S. Department of Health and Human Services, 2001)

Health Disparities: Hispanics/Latino/a Americans

38

- Hispanic/Latino/a Americans:
  - Prevalence rates of mental disorders in Mexican-born Mexican Americans similar to general population; however,
  - Prevalence rates for depression and phobias higher in U.S.-born Mexican Americans relative to European Americans
  - Limited data are available for some Latino/a groups (e.g., Cuban, Puerto Rican, Guatemalans, etc.)
  - The mental health service system fails to provide for the vast majority of Latinos/as in need of care
  - Latino/a immigrants have very limited access to mental health services
  - Latino/a youth are at high risk for poor mental health outcomes
  - Historical and sociocultural factors suggest Latinos/as are in great need of mental health services

(U.S. Department of Health and Human Services, 2001)

Research Challenges

39

It is "clearly recognized that psychology has been traditionally defined by and based upon Western, Eurocentric perspectives and assumptions that have governed the way in which research has been both conceptualized and implemented, including the general tendency to ignore the influence and impact of culture on cognition, emotion, and behavior. Thus, the effects of such biases have, at times, been detrimental to the diverse needs of the populations we serve and the public interest and have compromised our ability to accurately understand the people we serve."

(Council of National Psychological Associations, 2000, p. 1)

Weaknesses and Biases

- Lack of psychological research on ethnic minorities:
  - Examination of journal articles from 1970–1989 by Graham (1992) found only 3.6% included African Americans.
  - Iwamasa and Smith (1996) found only 1.3% of articles focused on U.S. ethnic minority groups.
  - Delgado-Romero, Gava, Maschino, and Rowland (2005) found that only 22% of research participants were from ethnic minority groups in a study of three counseling journals over 10 years.
- Generalizability of psychotherapeutic findings without cross-cultural validation.

Consensual Standards for Research With Cultural/Racial Populations

1. Use careful and detailed description of ethnicity/race/tribe in context of representative samples.
2. Recognize magnitude of within-group differences (heterogeneity).
3. Differentiate between impact of SES, race/ethnicity, and other potential confounds on research process and variables.
4. Assess and report acculturation status.
5. Examine effects of oppression in research process/outcome.
6. Recognize/investigate culture-specific communication styles and response sets.

Consensual Standards for Research With Cultural/Racial Populations (continued)

7. Understand cultural worldview effects upon research process/outcome.
8. Report participant language status and language fluency in context of required research tasks/instructions.
9. Include participation by culture-specific research consultants.
10. Address test equivalence in translations, constructs, and metric.
11. Use appropriate norms whenever available or caution in interpretation.
12. Use caution in interpreting differences from European Americans; avoid deficit-model interpretation.

(Council of National Psychological Associations, 2000; Kazdin, 2003)

Psychosocial Factors to Consider

- Group Differences Among Minority Groups
- Within-Group Differences-SES
- Acculturation Models
- Racial Identity Development
- Acculturation Status

CBMCS

Group Differences

CBMCS

Within-Group Differences

- Racial/ethnic identity development
- Cultural self
- Acculturation status
- Socioeconomic status

CBMCS

General Phases of Racial/Ethnic Identity Development Process

46

- Identifies with dominant culture:
  - May have internalized group stereotypes
  - May be unaware of cultural self
  - May deny or minimize cultural differences
- Experiences tension and conflict between one's own culture and dominant culture:
  - May have an "encounter" or "awakening" (e.g., becomes target of racism, attends meaningful cultural event)
  - Begins to have trouble resolving, minimizing group differences
- Identifies with own culture (culture of origin):
  - May immerse self in values, customs, traditions of own culture
  - May reject dominant cultural values
- Functions biculturally with comfortable cultural self-identity:
  - May work to address oppression and social injustice in all forms
  - May be comfortable, but selective, when in dominant culture relationships

(Helms & Cook, 1999)

CBMCS

Group, Individual, and Change Transformation Sources of Identity Formation

47

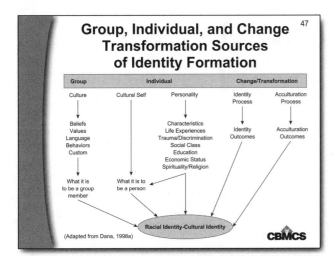

(Adapted from Dana, 1998a)

CBMCS

Cultural Self: Hispanic/Latino/a

48

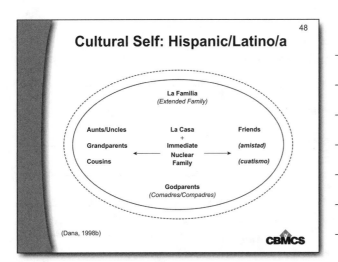

(Dana, 1998b)

CBMCS

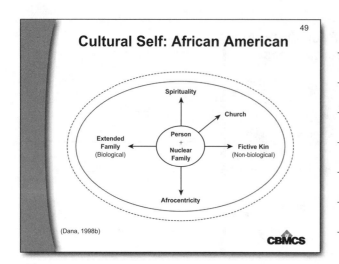

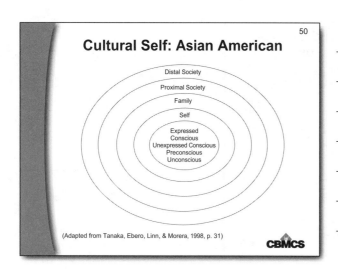

Cultural Self: Anglo American

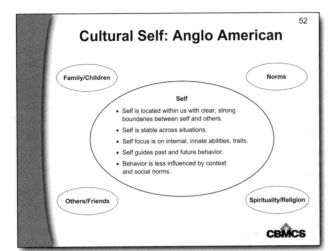

Family/Children

Norms

Self
- Self is located within us with clear, strong boundaries between self and others.
- Self is stable across situations.
- Self focus is on internal, innate abilities, traits.
- Self guides past and future behavior.
- Behavior is less influenced by context and social norms.

Others/Friends

Spirituality/Religion

CBMCS

Activity: Dialogue on Cultural Self

- Separate into self-selected ethnic/racial groups (Hispanic/ Latino, African American, Asian American, American Indian/Alaskan Native, European/Anglo American).
- Using the cultural self schema for your group, discuss how it does or does not apply to you.

CBMCS

Acculturation

- Psychological acculturation refers to how individuals adapt to the contact between two cultures.
- Different modes of acculturation may lead to more or less acculturation stress and better or worse psychological adjustment.
- Factors such as whether the culture change was voluntary or involuntary affect acculturation stress and adaptation.
- Characteristics of old culture and new culture affect acculturation stress and adaptation.

CBMCS

Modes of Acculturation

Important to Maintain Cultural Identity?

		No	Yes
Important to Relate to Dominant Group?	**No**	MARGINALIZATION *Lack identification with either group*	SEPARATION/ SEGREGATION *Chooses or is forced to withdraw from majority society*
	Yes	ASSIMILATION *Give up ethnic identity and adopt majority identity*	INTEGRATION *Maintain ethnic identity and incorporate majority identity*

(Berry, 1980)

CBMCS

Bicultural Integrated Identity and Mental Health

- Research shows bicultural individuals who are able to integrate their ethnic identity with mainstream identity tend to be better adjusted, have better coping skills, and demonstrate higher levels of achievement.
- Marginalized individuals tend to struggle in their social/economic attainment.

(LaFromboise, Coleman, & Gerton, 1993)

CBMCS

Acculturation Scales

- African American Acculturation Scale ([AAAS]; Landrine & Klonoff, 1994; [AAAS-R], Klonoff & Landrine, 2000)
- The Suinn-Lew Asian Self-Identity Scale (SL-ASIA; Suinn, Rickard-Figueroa, Lew, & Virgil, 1987)
- Acculturation Rating Scale for Mexican Americans II (ARSMA; Cuéllar, Arnold, & Maldonado, 1995; Cuéllar, Siles, & Bracamontes, 2004)
- Stephenson Multigroup Acculturation Scale (SMAS; Stephenson, 2000) Ethnic-general

CBMCS

Socioeconomic Status

- The effects of race and socioeconomic status on:
  - Identity, perspectives, problems, and behavior
  - Social standing: economic factors, prestige, and power
    - Ordinant groups
    - Subordinant groups
  - Within-group differences: racial/ethnic, social, and class
- Differential status identity

(Fouad & Brown, 2000)

CBMCS

Social Class

- Issues:
  - Research descriptions of subjects are faulty if European American comparative standard is used.
  - Use of SES flawed in comparisons due to interaction with racism/discrimination.
  - SES social class measures are deficient because of emphasis on income rather than differences in lifetime exposure to deprivation.
  - Percentages of ethnic minority groups below poverty line differ from European Americans.
  - Net worth of European Americans 13x African Americans.

(Dana, 1993)

CBMCS

Power Imbalance

- Differences between providers and consumers affecting relationships/ intervention outcomes:
  - Values
  - Health-illness beliefs
  - Expectations
  - Recognition of class differences

(Dana, 1998a)

CBMCS

Providing Culturally Competent Assessment, Diagnosis, and Treatment: Outline

- Limitations
- Multicultural Assessment and Intervention Process (MAIP)
- *DSM-IV-TR* Outline for Cultural Formulations
- Culture-Bound Syndromes
- Service Delivery Styles

Ethical Principles of Psychologists and Code of Conduct: Competence

2.01 Boundaries of Competence

(b) Where scientific or professional knowledge in the discipline of psychology establishes that an understanding of factors associated with age, gender, gender identity, race, ethnicity, culture, national origin, religion, sexual orientation, disability, language, or socioeconomic status is essential for effective implementation of their services or research, psychologists have or obtain the training, experience, consultation, or supervision necessary to ensure the competence of their services.

(American Psychological Association, 2002)

Ethical Principles of Psychologists and Code of Conduct: Assessment

9.06 Interpreting Assessment Results

When interpreting assessment results, including automated interpretations, psychologists take into account the purpose of the assessment as well as the various test factors, test-taking abilities, and other characteristics of the person being assessed, such as situational, personal, linguistic, and cultural differences, that might affect psychologists' judgments or reduce the accuracy of their interpretations. They indicate any significant limitations of their interpretations.

(American Psychological Association, 2002)

American Counseling Association: Diversity in Testing (E.8.)

Counselors are cautious in using assessment techniques, making evaluations, and interpreting the performance of populations not represented in the norm group on which an instrument was standardized. They recognize the effects of age, color, culture, disability, ethnic group, gender, race, religion, sexual orientation, and socioeconomic status on test administration and interpretation and place test results in proper perspective with other relevant factors. (See American Counseling Association, 2005.)

CBMCS

Deficiencies in Standard Assessment Protocols Across Cultures

- Test construction
  - Culture specific
  - U.S. and Western European based
- Test administration
  - High technology and low touch (medical model)

CBMCS

Deficiencies in Standard Assessment Protocols Across Cultures (continued)

- Test interpretation (assessor bias):
  - Distortion as a result of minimizing differences among people
  - Pathologized by labeling
  - Caricature as a result of stereotyping
  - Dehumanization as a result of inapplicable personality theories

CBMCS

Deficiencies in Standard Assessment Protocols Across Cultures (continued)

- Lack of consideration for social etiquette
- Lack of consideration for different cultural perspectives
- Failure to include culture specific tests
- The translation of an instrument does not necessarily mean that it is culturally appropriate

(Adapted from Dana, 2005, Table 1.1)

CBMCS

Bias: Sources and Corrections

Source	Bias	Correction
Clinician	Ethnocentrism Racism Prejudice Stereotyping	Examine own identity Immersion in another culture Training Supervision
Service delivery	European American Social etiquette: • Impersonal • Task oriented • Formal	Culture-specific styles of etiquette to show respect and facilitate compliance
Services: Test/ interventions	European American emics used as etics or pseudo-etics	Cross-cultural construct validity: equivalence in test language, format and content. Special group and acculturation status norms. New tests. Corrections for existing tests.
DSM-IV	European American emics Limited range of problem-specification	Cultural identity description Cultural self-description Culture-bound disorders (DSM-IV glossary)
Research	Methodology Research design Description of subjects	Consensual multicultural research standards

(Adapted from Dana, 2005, Table 1.1)

CBMCS

Implications for Treatment Service Delivery Style: African Americans

- Develop personal commonality in counseling relationship (when given permission); this may involve counselor self-disclosure, talking about noncounseling topics
- Expect humor, emotional expressiveness
- Expect spirituality, religious beliefs as part of identity
- Consider addressing racial differences and experiences with discrimination and racism directly (depending on stage of racial identity development)
- Find out expectations of counseling, worldviews, views of the problem
- Involve extended kinship network, community, church

(Dana, 1998a)

CBMCS

Implications for
Treatment Service Delivery Style:
African Americans (continued)

Seven African-Centered Values (*Nguzo Saba*):
- *Umoja* – unity
- *Kujichagulia* – self determination
- *Ujima* – collective work and responsibility
- *Ujamma* – cooperative economics
- *Nia* – purpose
- *Kuumbe* – creativity, fun
- *Imani* – spirituality and faith

(Dana, 1993)

Implications for Treatment Service
Delivery Style: Hispanic Americans

Cultural script for credible behavioral style:

- *Simpatía* (high frequencies of affiliative/affectional verbalizations)
- *Respeto* (respect by younger for older persons, women to men, persons in authority or higher socioeconomic position)
- *Personalismo/familismo* (preference for informal, personal, individualized attention)
- *Platicando* (leisurely chatting to establish a warm, accepting atmosphere)
- *Confianza en confianza* (mutual trust relationship, to establish mutual generosity, intimacy, personal involvement)

(Dana, 1993)

Implications for Treatment Service
Delivery Style: American
Indians/Alaskan Natives

1. Preassessment/treatment
   a. A preexisting social relationship with client in community will provide increased trust initially in assessment relationship.
2. Assessment/treatment setting
   a. With traditional person, chairs may be arranged next to one another to avoid immediate eye contact.
   b. Setting may be informal with other persons.
   c. Begin with informal chitchat on topics of mutual interest and shared understandings or "common basing."
   d. This "common basing" always includes an identification of mutual friends and acquaintances of both provider and client within a shared social frame of reference.

(Allen, 1998; Hornby, 1993)

Implications for Treatment Service Delivery Style: American Indians/Alaskan Natives (continued)

    e. The client needs to be satisfied that the provider not only has knowledge of his or her tribal history and group history as an Indian person in a genocidal society but also has a personal niche as an accepted person within the larger American Indian community.

    f. In the absence of these assurances, test data may be provided that are accepted by the client as reliable even though it is often minimal or guarded. Use of these data can result in overinterpretation that typically includes distortion, caricature and/or pathologization.

3. Postassessment/treatment

    a. Client can anticipate a continuing social relationship with the provider, preferably within community.

(Hornby, 1993)

Implications for Treatment Service Delivery Style: Asian Americans

1. Initiate relationship using cultural knowledge of proper social etiquette.
2. Demonstrate "credibility" and "gift-giving" (Sue & Zane, 1987).
    a. Credibility of role relationships (e.g., age, gender, expertise) depends on ascribed and achieved status of provider.
    b. Symbolic gift of immediate benefit (i.e., reduced anxiety, relief from depression, recognition that experiences are shared with others) strengthens relationship to facilitate subsequent services.
3. Recognize consumer use of alternative interventions (e.g., herbalist, acupuncturist, healers).
4. Emphasize structured, directive, goal-directed problem-solving approaches.

(Dana, 1993; Zane, Morton, Chu, & Lin, 2004)

Multicultural Assessment— Intervention Process (MAIP) Summary of Major Points

This model requires you to be mindful of
- Ethnic match
- Consumer acculturation/ethnic identity
- Staff cultural competence
- Ethnic specific/ general interventions
- Outcomes

(Costantino, Dana, & Malgady, 2007; Dana 2002a; also see Abreu, Gim Chung, & Atkinson, 2000, for discussion of various models)

DSM-IV Outline for Cultural Formulations

1. Cultural identity of the individual
2. Cultural explanation of the individual's illness
3. Cultural factors related to psychosocial environment and levels of functioning
4. Cultural elements of the relationship between the individual and the clinician
5. Overall cultural assessment for diagnosis and care

(American Psychiatric Association, 2000; Dana, 2002a; Costantino, Dana, & Malgady, 2007)

Corrections for Bias: *DSM-IV*

Classification System	Correction
1. Illness categories now reflect European American health/illness beliefs and erroneous conviction that many serious disorders are universal in their symptomatologies.	• Evolutionary change in successive *DSM* versions away from biological model (Castillo, 1997) and toward adequate incorporation of cultural issues in all illness categories (Mezzich, Kleinman, Fabrega, & Parron, 1996). • Routine use of cultural formulations increases reliability of diagnoses. • Recognition that diagnoses based on cultural self that differs from European American cultural self with rigid, relatively impermeable boundaries that largely exclude other persons as well as animals, spirits, and natural forces (Dana, 1998b). • Symptoms differ even for illness categories present in all groups (Dana, 2001).

Corrections for Bias: *DSM-IV* (continued)

Diagnostician Ineptness/Bias	Correction
• Inappropriate application of diagnoses due to failure of rapport whenever unacceptable style of service delivery is used as consequence of too little data or nonrepresentative consumer behaviors	• Training in credible, culture-specific social etiquette for service delivery.
• Insufficient knowledge of consumer cultural context and subsequent omission of cultural formulations required for accurate diagnosis.	• Training providers to use cultural formulations for consumers' traditional and marginal cultural orientation status.
• Lack of provider awareness of use of stereotypy or inadvertent racism.	• Training for provider self-awareness.

(Dana, 2002a)

Activity: Case Example

- Break into small groups.
- Spend 10 minutes reading and discussing case example.
- Do a cultural formulation by answering questions in the handout.

CBMCS

Examples of Culture-Bound Syndromes

1. *Ataque de nervios* among Hispanics (i.e., out-of-consciousness state resulting from evil spirits).
2. *Amok and mal de pelea* among clients from Malaysia, Laos, Philippines, Polynesia, Papua New Guinea, and Puerto Rico (a dissociative disorder involving outbursts of violent and aggressive or homicidal behavior directed at people and objects).
3. *Dhat* in the Indian, Chinese, and Sri Lankan communities (extreme anxiety associated with a sense of weakness, exhaustion, and the discharge of semen).

CBMCS

Examples of Culture-Bound Syndromes (continued)

4. *Falling-out* in African American communities (seizure-like symptoms resulting from traumatic events such as robberies).
5. *Ghost sickness* among American Indians (weakness and dizziness resulting from the action of witches and evil forces).
6. *Hwa-byung* in the Asian communities (pain in the upper abdomen, fear of death, and tiredness resulting from the imbalance between reality and anger).
7. *Koro* among Asians (a man's desire to grasp his penis resulting from the fear that it will retract into his body and cause death).

CBMCS

Examples of Culture-Bound Syndromes (continued)

8. *Pibloktog* in the case of clients from the Arctic and subarctic Eskimo communities (excitement, coma, and convulsive seizures resembling an abrupt dissociative episode, often associated with amnesia, withdrawal, irritability, and irrational behaviors such as breaking furniture, eating feces, and verbalization of obscenities).
9. *Taijin kyofusho* in the case of Asians (guilt about embarrassing others and timidity resulting from the feeling that the appearance, odor, or facial expressions are offensive to other people).

Examples of Culture-Bound Syndromes (continued)

10. *Mal puesto,* hex, root-work, and voodoo death among African Americans and Hispanics (unnatural diseases and death resulting from the power of people who use evil spirits).
11. *Susto, espanto, pasmo,* and *miedo* in the case of Hispanics (tiredness and weakness resulting from frightening and startling experiences).

(American Psychiatric Association, 2000; Griffith & Baker, 1993; Rubel, O'Nell, & Collado-Ardon, 1984; Stein, 1993)

Conclusion

Multicultural knowledge:
- Requires a personal commitment to be well informed about the communities we serve
- Requires a lifetime commitment
- Requires avoidance of simplistic characterizations of cultures
- Requires a personal commitment to be honest with oneself and accept what one does not know

(Personal communication, R. Guerrero, August 2005)

In Conclusion

85

CBMCS

Handouts

Module 1 Handout 1 (Slide 44)

Group Differences Among Minority Groups

Component	Group				
	European American	*African American*	*Hispanic American/ Latino/a*	*Asian American*	*American Indian/ Alaskan Native*
Personal identity	Individualistic self-concept	Sociocentric: extended self-concept includes other persons, originally nature/ spirit world	Sociocentric: extended self-concept (*la casa/la familia*)	Minimal individual self in family system context of priorities	Extended self-concept with fluid boundaries providing link to spirit and natural worlds
Group racial identity	Often poorly formed/ understood	Rearticulation of unconscious and everyday behaviors by rediscovery of origins and relearning what was once a coherent worldview (Afrocentrism)	Country of origin and familism (informal network of obligations, mutual support with family as attitudinal-behavioral refer)	Varies by group with Confucian, Buddhist, and Taoist values and behaviors	Identity amixture of traditional and Anglo components often conflicted
Language	English	English/Black English	Spanish/English	English/various	English and attempt to preserve/relearn many original non-Indo-European languages
Health/illness beliefs	Health = absence of disease Illness = organic/ psychological causes	Health as spiritual commitment to harmony between parts of self replaced by partial acceptance of Anglo beliefs	Traditionally: balance with God/harmony with family, others, customs of church plus spiritualism; increasing similarity to Anglo beliefs across generations	Health = balance/ harmony within family (yin-yang) Illness = physical, caused by bad spirits/curse/ punishment	Harmony/disharmony cycle; violation of sacred/ tribal taboos/ witchcraft as causes

| Component | Group | | | | |
	European American	African American	Hispanic American/Latino/a	Asian American	American Indian/Alaskan Native
Services	Individual focus	Group/family/community plus individual	Group/family/community plus individual	Focus within family system in which individual is secondary; home care/isolation	Group/community focus
Service provider	Professional/credentialized/highly paid; objective/rational/sympathetic/understanding	Friends, ministers, emergency room/hospital personnel first (not race); folk practitioners (rural) for spiritual/occult conditions	Traditional model: folk practitioner (no stigma/accept external causes); folk practitioners still acceptable for witchcraft/hexes	Professional/credentialized	Human qualities provide basis for trust/respect and willingness to receive services
Service delivery	Formal/professional relationships without dual roles	Accept as culturally understanding persons first; less separation of personal-professional roles	Proper social etiquette: *simpatía confianza en confianza, respeto, personalismo*; less role separation	Formal, role relationships with direct, practical focus	Rituals and traditional practices conducted in nonauthoritarian settings; dual roles required

SOURCE: Dana (1998a).

Module 1 Handout 2 (Slide 75)

MAIP Model

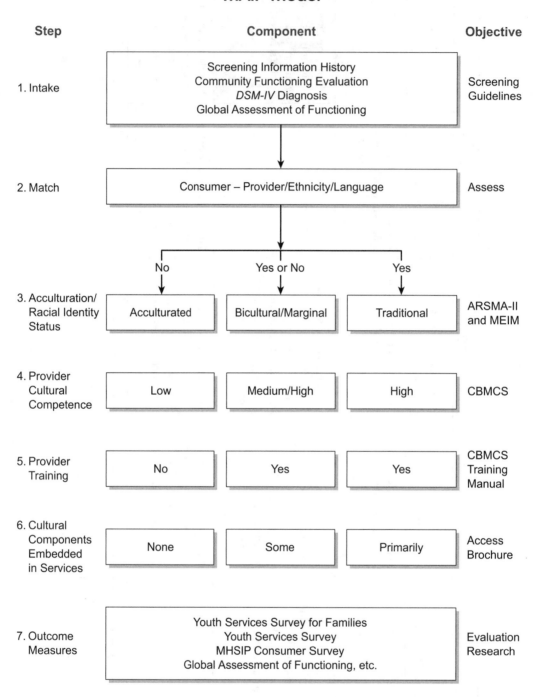

Step	Component	Objective
1. Intake	Screening Information History Community Functioning Evaluation *DSM-IV* Diagnosis Global Assessment of Functioning	Screening Guidelines
2. Match	Consumer – Provider/Ethnicity/Language	Assess
3. Acculturation/ Racial Identity Status	No → Acculturated Yes or No → Bicultural/Marginal Yes → Traditional	ARSMA-II and MEIM
4. Provider Cultural Competence	Low Medium/High High	CBMCS
5. Provider Training	No Yes Yes	CBMCS Training Manual
6. Cultural Components Embedded in Services	None Some Primarily	Access Brochure
7. Outcome Measures	Youth Services Survey for Families Youth Services Survey MHSIP Consumer Survey Global Assessment of Functioning, etc.	Evaluation Research

SOURCE: Dana, R. H., Aragon, M., & Kramer, T. (2002). *Public sector mental health services from multicultural populations: Bridging the gap from research to clinical practice.* Hauppauge, NY: Nova Science Publishers, Inc.

Module 1 Handout 3 (Slide 79)

Case Study: Emilio

Emilio is a 55-year-old evangelical preacher who emigrated from Mexico with his parents at the age of 5. He has been married for 30 years and has three adult children. He presented at the clinic because he was "feeling very anxious and not interested in usual activities." He requested that the interview be conducted in Spanish because he wanted to explain his situation using his "own language." This request was honored. Emilio has been an evangelistic preacher for over 30 years within various Latino communities. Approximately 6 months ago, he preached to an audience of about 500 Latinos, and during a moment of his speech, he began to feel ill, including difficulties breathing, trembling and shaking, sweating, and other symptoms, which "forced him" to seek medical help.

Emilio discussed this incident with his family, and they advised him to consult a physician. After several tests and procedures, he was told that "he is a healthy man, with no significant medical problems." His physician, a Latino familiar with Emilio's religious activities, also suggested that he seek a mental health professional, as his symptoms were perhaps psychological and not medical. Emilio did not immediately follow this recommendation because he wanted to wait to see if "God could give [him] the assurance that things will be okay" the next time he preached. However, he preached several times after his doctor's visit but continued to experience similar symptoms.

Emilio held his Bible during the discussion of his symptoms. When asked to think about events that contributed to his current feelings, he looked at his Bible for several seconds and acknowledged experiencing spiritual conflicts with God.

In particular, he knew that he should continue preaching but felt he needed a break after 30 years of preaching. Emilio reported that his conflict always surfaces each time he preaches from the podium. It is at that precise moment that his symptoms resemble a panic attack. He also becomes depressed at home when thinking about his spiritual conflicts with God.

When asked about his family, Emilio reported being content in his marriage and as a parent. His wife and extended family provide emotional support and encourage him to seek mental health treatment. The mental status evaluation indicated that Emilio was alert and oriented. He denied suicidal ideation or attempts. His thoughts appeared coherent and within the context expected by someone heavily involved in religious matters. Psychotic and delusional symptoms were not revealed during the intake.

Clinical Assessment

List the main *DSM-IV* diagnosis or diagnoses:

_____

_____

List the differential diagnosis or diagnoses:

_____

_____

List V-code(s) related to the disorder(s):

_____

_____

If this case does not meet criteria for a mental disorder, which specific V-code(s) would you consider as the focus of clinical attention and why?

_____

_____

Which cultural variables might be considered in the diagnosis and differential diagnosis of this case?

_____

_____

Cultural Formulation

Cultural identity of the client:

_____

_____

Cultural explanation of the individual's illness:

_____

_____

Cultural factors related to psychosocial environment and level of functioning:

_____

_____

Cultural elements of the relationship between the client and the clinician:

_____

_____

Overall cultural assessment for diagnosis and care of the present mental disorder:

_____

_____

SOURCE: From Paniagua, F. A. (2001). *Diagnosis in a multicultural context: A casebook for mental health professionals.* Thousand Oaks, CA: Sage Publications.

References

Abreu, J. M., Gim Chung, R. H., & Atkinson, D. R. (2000). Multicultural counseling training: Past, present and future directions. *The Counseling Psychologist, 28,* 641–656.

Allen, J. (1998). Personality assessment with American Indians and Alaska Natives: Instrument considerations and service delivery style. *Journal of Personality Assessment, 70,* 17–42.

American Psychiatric Association. (2000). *Diagnostic and statistical manual of mental disorders: DSM-IV-TR* (4th ed., text revision). Washington DC: Author.

American Psychological Association. (2002). *Ethical principles of psychologists and code of conduct.* Retrieved November 2, 2007, from www.apa.org/ethics/code2002.html#2_01

Arredondo, P., & Arciniega, G. M. (2001). Strategies and techniques for counselor training based on the multicultural counseling competencies. *Journal of Multicultural Counseling and Development, 29,* 263–273.

Bennett, M. J. (1986). A developmental approach to training the intercultural sensitivity. *International Journal of Intercultural Relations, 10,* 179–196.

Berry, J. (1980). Acculturation as variety of adaptation. In A. M. Padilla (Ed.), *Acculturation: Theory, model, and some new findings* (pp. 9–25). Boulder, CO: Westview Press.

California State Department of Finance, Demographic Research Unit. (2001, March). *Current population survey report.* Sacramento: Author.

Castillo, R. J. (1997). *Culture and mental illness: A client-centered approach.* Pacific Grove, CA: Brooks/Cole.

Choney, S. K., Berryhill-Paapke, E., & Robbins, R. R. (1995). The acculturation of American Indians: Developing frameworks for research and practice. In J. G. Ponterotto, J. M. Casa, L. A. Suzuki, & C. M. Alexander (Eds.), *Handbook of multicultural counseling* (pp. 73–92). Thousand Oaks, CA: Sage.

Christian, C. M. (1999). *Black saga: The African American experience, a chronology.* Washington, DC: Civitas Counterpoint.

Comas-Diaz, L. (2000). Hispanic, Latinos, or Americanos: The evolution of identity. *Cultural Diversity and Ethnic Minority Psychology, 7,* 115–120.

Constantine, M. G., & Sue, D. W. (2005). The American psychological Association's Guidelines on multicultural education, training, research, practice, and organizational psychology: Initial development and summary. In M. G. Constantine & Sue (Eds.), *Strategies for building multicultural competence in mental health and educational settings* (pp. 3–15). New York: Wiley.

Costantino, G., Dana, R. H., & Malgady, R. G. (2007). *TEMAS (Tell-Me-A-Story) Assessment in multicultural societies.* Mahwah, NJ: Erlbaum.

Council of National Psychological Associations for the Advancement of Ethnic Minority Interests. (2000). *Guidelines for research in ethnic minority communities.* Washington DC: American Psychological Association.

Cross, T. Bazron, B., Dennis, K., & Isaacs, M. (1989). *Towards a culturally competent system of care* (Vol. I). Washington DC: Georgetown University Child Development Center, CASSP Technical Assistance Center.

Cuéllar, I., Arnold, B., & Maldonado, R. (1995). Acculturation rating scale for Mexican Americans-II: A revision of the original ARSMA Scale. *Hispanic Journal of Behavioral Sciences, 17,* 275–304.

Cuéllar, I., Siles, R., & Bracamontes, E. (2004). Acculturation: A psychological construct of continuing relevance for Chicana/o psychology. In R. Velasquez, L. Arellano, & B. McNeill (Eds.), *The handbook of Chicana/o psychology and mental health* (pp. 23–42). Mahwah, NJ: Erlbaum.

Dana, R. H. (1993). *Multicultural assessment perspectives for professional psychology.* Boston: Allyn & Bacon.

Dana, R. H. (1998a). *Understanding cultural identity in intervention and assessment.* Thousands Oaks, CA: Sage.

Dana, R. H. (1998b). The cultural self: Etic and emic contexts as learning resources. In L. Handler & M. Hilsenroth (Eds.), *Teaching and learning personality assessment* (pp. 325–345). Hillsdale, NJ: Erlbaum.

Dana, R. H. (2000a). The cultural self as locus for assessment and intervention with American Indians/Alaska Natives. *Journal of Multicultural Counseling and Development, 28,* 66–82.

Dana, R. H. (2001). Clinical diagnosis of multicultural populations in the United States. In L. A. Suzuki, J. G. Ponterotto, & P. J. Meller (Eds.), *The handbook of multicultural assessment* (2nd ed., pp. 101–131). San Francisco: Jossey-Bass.

Dana, R. H. (2002a). Examining the usefulness of *DSM-IV.* In K. Kurasaki, S. Okazaki, & S. Sue (Eds.), *Asian American mental health: Assessment, theories, and methods* (pp. 1–20). Dordrecht, Netherlands: Kluwer Academic.

Dana, R. H. (2002b). Mental health services for African Americans: A cultural/racial perspective. *Cultural Diversity and Ethnic Minority Psychology, 8,* 3–18

Dana, R. H. (2005). *Multicultural assessment: Principles, applications and examples.* Mahwah, NJ: Erlbaum.

Dana, R. H. (2007). Clinical diagnosis of multicultural populations. In L. A. Suzuki, J. G. Ponterotto, & U. F. Meller (Eds.), *Handbook of multicultural assessment: Clinical, psychological, and educational applications* (3rd ed., pp. 107–131). San Francisco: Jossey-Bass.

Dana, R. H., Aragon, M., & Kramer, T. (2002). *Public sector mental health services from multicultural populations: Bridging the gap from research to clinical practice.* Hauppauge, NY: Nova Science Publishers, Inc.

Feagin, J. R., & Feagin, C. B. (1999). *Racial and ethnic relations* (6th ed.). Upper Saddle River, NJ: Prentice Hall.

Fouad, N. A., & Brown, M. T. (2000). Role of race and social class in development: Implications for counseling psychology. In S. D. Brown & R. W. Lent (Eds.), *Handbook of counseling Psychology* (pp. 379–408). New York: Wiley.

Gamst, G., Dana, R. H., Der-Karabetian, A., Aragon, M., Arellano, L. Morrow, G., & Martenson, L. (2004). Cultural competence revised: The California Brief Multicultural Competence Scale. *Measurement and Evaluation in Counseling and Development, 37,* 163–187.

Griffith, E. H., & Baker, F. M. (1993). Psychiatric care of African Americans. In A. C. Gaw (Ed.), *Culture, ethnicity and mental illness* (pp. 147–173). Washington, DC: American Psychiatric Press.

Guthrie, R. A. (1976). *Even the rat was white: A historical view of psychology.* New York: Bantam.

Hammer, M. R., Bennett, M. J., & Wiseman, R. (2003). Measuring intercultural sensitivity: The Intercultural Development Inventory. *International Journal of Intercultural Relations, 27,* 421–443.

Helms, J., & Cook, D. (1999). *Using race and culture in counseling and psychotherapy: Theory and practice.* Boston: Allyn & Bacon.

Hornby, R. (1993). *Competency training for human service providers.* Mission, SD: Gleska Press.

Isaacs, M. R., & Benjamin, M. P. (1991). *Towards a culturally competent system of care* (Vol. II). Washington, DC: Georgetown University, CASSP Technical Assistance Center.

Kazdin, A. E. (2003). *Research design in clinical psychology* (4th ed.). Boston: Allyn & Bacon.

Klonoff, E. A., & Landrine, H. (2000). Revising and improving the African American Acculturation Scale. *Journal of Black Psychology, 26,* 235–261.

LaFromboise, T., Coleman, H. L. K., & Gerton, J. (1993). Psychological impact of biculturalism: Evidence and theory. *Psychological Bulletin, 114,* 395–412.

Lam, A. G., & Sue, S. (2001). Client diversity. *Psychotherapy, 38,* 479–486.

Landrine, H., & Klonoff, E. A. (1994). The African American Acculturation Scale. *Journal of Black Psychology, 20,* 104–127.

Locke, D. C. (1998). *Increasing multicultural understanding.* Thousand Oaks, CA: Sage.

Mezzich, J. E., Kleinman, A., Fabrega, H. Jr., & Parron, D. L. (Eds.). (1996). *Culture and psychiatric diagnosis: A DSM-IV perspective.* Washington, DC: American Psychiatric Press.

Microsoft Encarta Online Encyclopedia. (1998). *Mexican Americans.* Retrieved October 11, 2007, from http://encarta.msn.com/encyclopedia_761587500/Mexican_Americans.html

Paniagua, F. A. (2001). *Diagnosis in a multicultural context: A casebook for mental health professionals.* Thousand Oaks, CA: Sage.

Pope-Davis, D. B., Coleman, H. L. K., Liu, W. M., & Toporek, R. L. (2003). *Handbook of multicultural competencies in counseling and psychology.* Thousand Oaks, CA: Sage.

Rubel, A. J., O'Nell, C. W., & Collado-Ardon, R. (1984). *Susto: A folk illness.* Berkeley: University of California Press.

Stein, D. J. (1993). Cross-cultural psychiatry, and the DSM-IV. *Comprehensive Psychiatry, 34,* 322–329.

Stephenson, M. (2000). Development and validation of the Stephenson Multigroup Acculturation Scale (SMAS). *Psychological Assessment, 12, 77–88.*

Sue, D. W., & Zane, N. W. S. (1987). The role of culture and cultural techniques in psychotherapy: A critique and reformulation. *American Psychologist, 42, 37–45.*

Suinn, R. M., Rickard-Figueroa, K., Lew, S., & Virgil, S. (1987). The Suinn-Lew Asian Self-Identity Acculturation scale: An initial report. *Educational and Psychological Measurement, 47,* 401–407.

Tanaka, J. S., Ebero, A., Linn, B., & Morera, O. F. (1998). Research methods: The construct validity of self-identity and its psychological implications. In L. C. Lee & N. W. S. Zane (Eds.), *Handbook of Asian American psychology* (pp. 21–79). Thousand Oaks, CA: Sage.

Triandis, H. C., Marin, G., Lisansky, J., & Betancourt, H. (1984). Simpatia as a cultural script of Hispanics. *Journal of personality and Social Psychology, 47,*1363–1375.

U.S. Department of Health and Human Services. (2001). *Mental health: Culture, race, and ethnicity: A supplement to mental health: A report of the surgeon general—Executive summary.* Rockville, MD: Author.

Zane, N., Morton, T. Chu, J., & Lin, N. (2004). Counseling and psychotherapy with Asian American Clients. In T. B. Smith (Ed.), *Practicing multiculturalism: Affirming diversity in counseling and psychology* (pp. 190–214). Boston: Allyn & Bacon.

AWARENESS OF CULTURAL BARRIERS

Slides

Module 2
Awareness of Cultural Barriers

CBMCS

Acknowledgments

Richard H. Dana, Regional Research Institute for
Human Services, Portland State University
Glenn C. Gamst, University of La Verne
Aghop Der-Karabetian, University of La Verne

With Contributions From
Leticia Arellano-Morales, University of La Verne
Marya Endriga, Califordenia State University, Sacramento
Robbin Huff-Musgrove, San Bernardino County Department of
Behavioral Health
Gloria Morrow, Private Practice

With Generous Support From
California Department of Mental Health–Office of
Multicultural Services
Eli Lilly Foundation
California Mental Health Directors Association
California Institute of Mental Health
University of La Verne, La Verne, CA

CBMCS

Introductions

CBMCS

Module 2 Overview

1. Highlights
2. Context of Barriers
3. Awareness of Self
   a. Cultural Self-Awareness
   b. Worldview
   c. Racial/Ethnic Identity
4. Awareness of Others
   a. Oppression
   b. Racism
   c. Privilege
   d. Gender Differences
   e. Sexual Orientations
5. Clinical Implications

CBMCS

Context of Barriers to Care

- Consumer challenges
- Conflict in consumer-provider cultural values
- Power differentials
- Institutional barriers to services
- Personal beliefs and stereotypes

CBMCS

Goals and Objectives

- To become aware of personal values, beliefs, and ethnic/racial/cultural background
- To become aware of the effects of discrimination and oppression
- To become aware of privilege, bias, and stereotypes
- To become aware of service delivery implications
- To apply self-awareness to the repertoire of multicultural skills

CBMCS

Activity: Multicultural Knowledge

1. What is culture?
2. What is race?
3. What is ethnicity?
4. What is acculturation?
5. What is cultural competence?
6. What does cultural competence have to do with clinical competence?

CBMCS

What Is Culture?

Culture is the set of attitudes, values, beliefs, symbols, and behaviors shared by a group of people, but different for each individual, and usually communicated from one generation to the next.

(Dana, 1998; Sue & Sue, 2003)

CBMCS

What Is Race?

Race is a social category, and cultures classify persons into racial groups on the basis of socially significant characteristics. Race is no longer considered a biological category because greater variation occurs within racial groups than between these groups.

(Dana, 1998; Sue & Sue, 2003)

CBMCS

What Is Ethnicity?

Ethnicity refers to possession of a common heritage historically. This heritage includes behaviors, beliefs, customs, language, and symbols.

(Dana, 1998; Sue & Sue, 2003)

CBMCS

What Is Acculturation?

Acculturation is the process and outcome of selective socialization of an individual from an original culture to the dominant or host culture.

(Dana, 1998; Sue & Sue, 2003)

CBMCS

What Is Cultural Competence?

Cultural competence is the state of being capable of functioning effectively in the context of cultural differences. It operates at individual and institutional levels and is a developmental process.

(Ponterotto, Casas, Suzuki, & Alexander, 2001)

CBMCS

What Does Cultural Competence Have to Do With Clinical Competence?

Cultural competence increases the likelihood that clinical services (i.e., assessment, diagnosis, treatment) are culturally appropriate, that mental health utilization rates will increase for minority groups, and that the overall quality of services and outcomes will be improved.

(Bernal, Trimble, Burlew, & Leong, 2003)

CBMCS

Self-Awareness Overview

Self-Awareness Definition

Worldview

Racial/Ethnic Identity Models

CBMCS

Self-Awareness Definition

- Self-awareness involves the myriad ways that culture affects human behavior.
- Self-awareness involves recognizing how one's cultural background, experiences, attitudes, values, biases, and emotional reactions influence psychological processes.
- Self-awareness helps us to recognize the limits of our competencies and expertise.

(Sue & Sue, 2003)

CBMCS

Cultural Self-Awareness

- Who Are You? (WAY) (Dana, 2005)
- *Conocimiento* (self-knowledge) activity
- Worldview and values (Scale to Assess Worldview; SAWV) (Ibrahim & Kahn, 1987)

CBMCS

Activity: Who Are You?

1. Please complete the WAY worksheet
2. Next to your responses:
   - Star the ones most important to your identity.
   - Write "P" next to personality descriptions.
   - Write "R" next to roles or relationships.
   - Write "C" next to responses related to culture.
3. Look for patterns:
   - More personality or role responses or equal?
   - Are cultural responses also personality or role responses or both?

(Dana, 2005)

CBMCS

Activity: *Conocimiento*

Sample questions:
- What is your full birth name? What meaning does it have in your family?
- How many in your family?
- Where were you born?
- Where were your parents born?
- What is your family's country of origin?
- What is your primary language? Languages spoken in your family
- What's one thing we'd never guess about you?

CBMCS

Definition of Worldview

19

- Worldviews represent beliefs, values, and assumptions about people, relationships, nature, time, and activity in our world. (Ibrahim, Roysircar-Sodowsky, & Ohnishi, 2001)
- Worldviews affect how we perceive and evaluate situations and how we derive appropriate actions based on our appraisal.
- The nature of clinical reality is also linked to one's worldviews.

(Sue & Sue, 2003)

CBMCS

Worldview Dimensions

20

Worldviews have a set of core dimensions that pertain to peoples of all cultures:

- Time Focus
- Human Activity
- Social Relations
- People/Nature Relationship

(Ibrahim, 1985; Kluckhohn & Strodtbeck, 1961)

CBMCS

Worldview Dimensions: Time Focus

21

What is the temporal focus of human life?

- Past: The past is important. Learn from history.
- Present: The present moment is everything. Don't worry about tomorrow.
- Future: Plan for the future. Sacrifice today for a better tomorrow.

(Sue & Sue, 2003)

CBMCS

Worldview Dimensions: Human Activity

What is the modality of human activity?
- <u>Being:</u> It's enough just to be.
- <u>Being and in-becoming:</u> Our purpose in life is to develop our inner self.
- <u>Doing:</u> Be active. Work hard and your efforts will be rewarded.

(Sue & Sue, 2003)

Worldview Dimensions: Social Relations

How are human relationships defined?
- <u>Lineal:</u> Relationships are vertical. There are leaders and followers in the world.
- <u>Collateral:</u> We should consult with friends/families when problems arise.
- <u>Individualistic:</u> Autonomy is important. We control our own destiny.

(Sue & Sue, 2003)

Worldview Dimensions: People/Nature Relationship

What is the relationship of people to nature?
- <u>Subjugation to nature:</u> Life is largely determined by external forces (e.g., God).
- <u>Harmony with nature:</u> People and nature coexist in harmony.
- <u>Mastery over nature:</u> Our challenge is to conquer and control nature.

(Sue & Sue, 2003)

Racial/Ethnic Identity

- Refers to the part of personal identity that contributes to one's self-image as an ethnic member or one's subjective experience of ethnicity.
- Racial identity reflects the psychological consequences of racial socialization.

(Trimble, Helms, & Root, 2003)

Racial Identity

Incident

Once riding in old Baltimore,
    Heart-filled, head-filled with glee,
I saw a Baltimorean
    Keep looking straight at me,

Now I was eight and very small,
    And he was no whit bigger,
And so I smiled, but he poked out
    His tongue and called me, "Nigger."

I saw the whole of Baltimore
    From May until December;
Of all the things that happened there
    That's all that I remember.

        — Countee Cullen (1927)

Source: *On These I Stand: An Anthology of the Best Poems of Countee Cullen*, by Countee Cullen, Harper & Brothers, 1947.

Racial/Cultural Identity Development (R/CID): Minority Group Model

Stage 1: Conformity	Prefers dominant culture values; may hold negative view of own culture
Stage 2: Dissonance	Questions previous beliefs; increasing awareness of racism; emergent cultural pride conflicts with dominant view
Stage 3: Resistance and immersion	Rejects dominant values; immerses self in cultural activities; feels shame at previous beliefs
Stage 4: Introspection	Realizes need for personal autonomy within cultural identity; less intensity and rigidity than Stage 3
Stage 5: Integrative awareness	Appreciates own culture and aspects of dominant culture; experiences less conflict; commits to social justice activities to fight oppression

(Atkinson, Morten, & Sue, 1998)

Racial/Cultural Identity Development (R/CID): White/European American Model

Stage 1: Conformity	Holds ethnocentric attitudes; relies on social stereotypes; believes (consciously or unconsciously) in white superiority; color-blind "people are people" belief
Stage 2: Dissonance	Confronts own personal biases, prejudices and sees racism; may attempt to rationalize guilt, anger
Stage 3: Resistance and immersion	Sees racism everywhere and challenges own racism; may feel negatively about being white; may swing back to conformity to deal with discomfort
Stage 4: Introspection	Becomes less motivated by guilt; accepts own whiteness; asks, "What does it mean to be white?"
Stage 5: Integrative awareness	Forms nonracist white identity; appreciates diversity; commits to fighting oppression

(Sue & Sue, 2003)

CBMCS

Culture-Specific Racial/Cultural Identity Development Models and Measures

- <u>African American:</u> Cross (1991, 1995); Cross and Vandiver (2001)
- <u>Asian American:</u> Sodowsky, Kwan, and Pannu (1995); Suinn, Ahuna, and Kloo (1992)
- <u>European/White American:</u> Helms and Carter (1990)
- <u>Hispanic/Latino American:</u> Casas and Pytluk (1995); Cuéllar, Arnold, and Maldonado (1995); Ruiz (1990)
- <u>Native American:</u> Bates, Beauvais, and Trimble (1997); Dana (1998, Table 4.3, p. 75); Lysne and Levy (1997); Zimmerman, Ramirez-Valles, Washienki, Walter, and Dyer (1996)

CBMCS

Activity: Racial/Cultural Identity Development

	C	D	RI	I	IA
C	—	1	2	3	4
D	5	—	6	7	8
RI	9	10	—	11	12
I	13	14	15	—	16
IA	17	18	19	20	—

CBMCS

Awareness of Others

31

Expression of Power

Oppression

Racism

A Difference of Color

Gender Differences

Sexual Orientation

CBMCS

Expression of Power

32

- Power is associated with authority, control, dominance, mastery, strength, and superiority.
- Undergirds status, increases access to desired goals, achievement, possessions, independence, etc.
- Consumer-provider power differential.
- Positional power, personal power, legitimate authority.
- Class dominance: Power is concentrated in a small group of individuals who compose a power elite.
- Those who have power are the gatekeepers of resources (e.g., mental health services, health care, employment, and educational opportunities).

(Arendt, 1970; Pinderhughes, 1989)

CBMCS

Oppression

33

An act (or acts) of violence that by its nature interferes with a person's ability to evolve as a complete human being. Also includes any attempt to exploit or hinder others in their pursuits of self-determination.

(Freire, 1970)

CBMCS

Five Faces of Oppression

- <u>Exploitation:</u> efforts of one group get transferred into benefits to another group
- <u>Marginalization:</u> exclusion of groups from labor and other benefits resulting in deprivation
- <u>Powerlessness:</u> exclusion from decision-making processes that affect one's quality of life
- <u>Cultural imperialism:</u> assumption that dominant cultural norms represent all humanity
- <u>Violence toward individuals:</u> systematic physical or psychological violence because they are members of an oppressed group

(Young, 2001)

Difficulties in Discussing Oppression

- Issues of oppression or racism are often difficult to discuss, particularly for informed and experienced white therapists (Hansen et al., 2006).
- Due to the pain, and hurt, clients may deny, rationalize, or avoid discussing their feelings/belief regarding race and ethnicity.
- When these feelings are not expressed, therapists may be uncomfortable initiating discussions of racial/ethnic differences for fear of offending or due to color-blind attitudes (Cardemil & Battle, 2003; Maxie, Arnold, & Stephenson, 2006; Utsey, Gernat, & Hammar, 2005).
- As a consequence, the process and outcome of psychotherapy is affected and healing may be compromised. Practicing cultural empathy (Ridley & Lingle, 1996) facilitates these discussions and specific considerations can be helpful (La Roche & Maxie, 2003).

CBMCS

Effects of Oppression

- Alienation
- Denial of resources
- Cruel or unjust treatment
- Loss of language and culture
- Pathologization of ethnic/racial communities
- Poverty

CBMCS

Definition of Racism

Racism is defined as "a complex aggregate of prejudice and discrimination based on an ideology of racial domination and oppression."

(Essed, 1990)

Racism

Occurs in circumstances where members of a dominant group create or accept their societal privilege by "maintaining structures, ideology, values, and behavior that have the intent or effect of leaving nondominant-group members relatively excluded from power, esteem, status, and/or equal access to societal resources."

(Harrell, 2000, p. 43)

Types of Racism

Definitions

- Individual racism – Individual attitudes, beliefs, and actions that support or perpetuate racism

    Experienced on a personal level

- Institutional racism – Social institutions that support or perpetuate racism

    Experienced as a result of racism being embedded in the policies of a given institution

- Cultural racism – The belief that cultural practices of one group are superior to those of another

    Results from the cultural practices of one group being lauded as superior to those of another

(Harrell, 2000; Jones, 1997)

Types of Racism (continued)

- Environmental racism – Sanctioning of policies and laws that allow for the life-threatening presence of poisons or pollutants in communities of color
- Collective racism – Formally organizing to restrict the rights of persons of color
- Modern racism – A subtle form of bias characteristic of many Americans who possess strong egalitarian values and who believe that they are not prejudiced

When organized/semi-organized whites seek to restrict the rights of ethnic minorities or immigrants

(Harrell, 2000)

CBMCS

Video Clip Selection

CBMCS

Acute Racism Reactions

1. Racism-related fatigue – Psychological and physiological exhaustion experienced in response to chronic exposure to racism and oppression
2. Anticipatory racism reaction – Development of defense mechanisms due to being the victim or recipient of racial discrimination or racially motivated hostility

(Clark, Anderson, Clark, & Williams, 1999; Utsey, Bolden, & Brown, 2001)

CBMCS

Acute Racism
Reactions (continued)

3. Race-related stress/distress – Acute stressors due to encounters with racism and oppression that may manifest physically or psychologically
4. Racism-related frustration – Frustration resulting from racial incidents

(Utsey, Bolden, & Brown, 2001)

Acute Racism
Reactions (continued)

5. Racism-related confusion – The search for identity due to racist exchanges, causing confusion, bewilderment, and psychological and physical fatigue

(Utsey, Bolden, & Brown, 2001)

Physiological Effects of Racism

- Hypertension
- Cardiovascular reactivity
- Physiological arousal
- Increased susceptibility to minor and major illness due to a weakened immune system

(Harrell, 2000)

Racism as a Clinical Syndrome?

Due to the deleterious effects of racism, it has been proposed that racism should be considered a clinical syndrome as it encompasses an etiology and clinical taxonomy.

(Dobbins & Skillings, 2000)

CBMCS

Activity: Self-Assessment

Self-Assessment of Readiness

CBMCS

How Does Racism Impact the Clinical Setting?

CBMCS

A Difference of Color

CBMCS

Skin Color Privilege

Skin color privilege results from an identifiable racial hierarchy that creates a system of social advantages or "special rights" primarily on race rather than merit. Certain persons/groups are assumed to be entitled to more than an equitable share in the allocation of resources and opportunities. These unearned advantages are invisible and often unacknowledged by those who benefit.

(McIntosh, 2000; Neville, Worthington, & Spanierman, 2001)

CBMCS

White Privilege

White Americans enjoy extra degrees of freedom, or a set of special unearned privileges, that they can tap into every day of their lives.

(McIntosh, 1989)

CBMCS

White Privilege (continued)

- Racial identity reflects one's socialization.
- White privilege is related to an individual's ethnic/racial identity development.
- Helms suggests a developmental process through which whites can move to recognize and abandon their privilege.

(Helms, 1990)

White Privilege (continued)

- Individuals operating primarily at Helms's contact status tend to be oblivious to racism.
- immersion/emersion status individuals search for an understanding how they benefit from racism.
- Autonomy status individuals develop the capacity to relinquish their privileges of racism.

(Helms, 1990; Trimble, Helms, & Root, 2003)

Activity: On Privilege

- I can if I wish arrange to be in the company of people of my race most of the time.
- I can turn on the television or open to the front page of the paper and see people of my race widely represented.
- If a traffic cop pulls me over, I can be sure I haven't been singled out because of my race.

(McIntosh, 1989)

Activity: On Privilege (continued)

55

- I have never been asked to speak for all people in my racial group.
- I have the ability to ensure that my children are provided with curricular materials that testify to the existence of their race.

(McIntosh, 1989)

Examples of White Privilege

56

On average, whites are more likely than members of racial-ethnic minority groups to experience the following:
- Attend schools with smaller class sizes with early access to school/home computers
- Graduation from 4-year college/university
- Higher salaries; increased job security

(McIntosh, 1989)

Examples of White Privilege (continued)

57

- Health insurance, more frequent recovery from certain life-threatening diseases
- Favorable housing conditions, unimpeded access to home mortgage loans, and smaller percentage of income expended on housing
- Ownership of mutual funds, stocks, IRA/Keogh accounts

(McIntosh, 1989)

Examples of White Privilege (continued)

Criminal Justice System:

- White males receive less severe sentences than black and Latino males.
- White defendants who harm whites receive milder penalties than blacks who harm whites.
- Blacks are incarcerated six times more than whites.

(Spohn, 2000)

Examples of White Privilege (continued)

Mental Health:

Compared with ethnic minority groups, whites…
- receive more accurate mental health diagnoses,
- have better access to larger variety of treatment settings (outpatient vs. inpatient),
- are less likely to drop out of treatment prematurely,
- receive more up-to-date medications.

(Substance Abuse and Mental Health Services Administration, 2001)

Possible Outcomes of Increased Knowledge of White Privilege

- Heightened awareness
- Guilt or shame
- Shock
- Cognitive dissonance
- Fear and loss related to relinquishing unearned privileges
- Possible negative consequences from other whites

Sexism

CBMCS

Definition of Sexism

Prejudice or discrimination based on sex.

It is the belief that women and men are innately different and that those innate differences translate into female inferiority.

(Marger, 2005)

CBMCS

Sexism

- Men can assume that when they go out in public, they won't be sexually harassed or assaulted. If they are victimized, they won't be asked to explain what they were doing there.
- Women can be revictimized in mental health treatment.
- Men can succeed without others' being surprised.
- Men hold higher positions of power and privilege in business and government.

CBMCS

Heterosexual Bias

Heterosexism

Heterosexism is "a belief in the inherent superiority of one pattern of loving over all others and thereby its right to dominance."

(Audre Lorde, cited in Rashid, 2007)

Heterosexual Privilege

- Being free to reveal and live intimate relationships openly, by referring to partners by name, going out in public together, and displaying pictures on one's desk without being accused of "flaunting" one's sexuality.
- Heterosexual marriages are legally recognized, thus allowing couples to receive various fringe benefits (health insurance, alimony, etc.).

Heterosexual Privilege
(continued)

- Heterosexuals are able to view multimedia and see characters reflective of their own heterosexual orientation.
- Heterosexuals do not fear that their sexual orientation will be used as a weapon against them to undermine their achievements or power.

(Johnson, 2001)

CBMCS

Activity: Culturally Competent and Incompetent Role-Play

Some Awareness Themes to Consider:
- Provider understanding (or lack of) different worldviews or imposing one's own
- Provider awareness (or lack of) of differences in ethnic identity between self and consumer
- Provider acknowledging or denying existence of oppression and racism and its effects
- Provider awareness (or lack of) of power differentials and personal privileges

CBMCS

Multicultural Awareness

CBMCS

MODULE 2—AWARENESS OF CULTURAL BARRIERS

Benefits of Multicultural Awareness

- Proactive multicultural sensitivity and responsiveness
- Advocacy within institutions
- Increased ability to work in multicultural settings
- Improved clinical outcomes
- More effective evaluation/assessment
- Enjoyment of multiculturalism
- Increased access to services for racial/ethnic/cultural groups

Advocacy and Outreach

- Mental health providers as social change agents
- Advocacy stance for changes in social institutions
- Consumer provider partnerships
- Empowerment to restore distorted or deprived personal biography, collective history
- Legislation to ensure equity
- Community interventions: Empowerment via collective responsiveness/actions

(Comas-Diaz, Lykes, & Alarcon, 1998)

Clinical Implications

Clinical Implications

- Multicultural awareness helps to ensure that appropriate assessment, diagnosis, and treatment are provided to culturally diverse consumers.
- Provider self-awareness is important for improving clinical outcomes because providers and consumers exchange worldviews, values, attitudes, beliefs, and experiences as part of the therapeutic process.
- Self-awareness assists in improving the overall quality of services.

CBMCS

Clinical Interventions

- Establish a therapeutic relationship that acknowledges cultural differences.
- Use credible service delivery styles that demonstrate respect.
- Use culture-specific elements (emic) combined with culture-general (etic) interventions (MAIP model).

(Dana, 1998)

CBMCS

Clinical Interventions (continued)

- Use culture-specific interventions with traditional, bicultural, and marginal persons for oppression-related problems (MAIP model).
- Use multiple roles and advocacy stance with consumers.
- Understand when it is mandatory to match providers and consumers for race/ethnicity.

(Dana, 1998)

CBMCS

Activity: Culture-Specific Intervention

1. Read and discuss assigned vignette in small groups.
2. Discuss multicultural issues present in the interview.
3. Discuss possible barriers to consider when working with this client and strategies to overcome those barriers.

(Geller, 1988)

CBMCS

Conclusion

CBMCS

Handouts

Module 2 Handout 1 (Slide 16)

Who Are You? (WAY)

1. Trainees should first complete the WAY.

2. All trainees should read their copy of the sample WAY from a young Korean American woman.

3. Group discussion of cultural contents in WAY response sample. For interpretation, it may be assumed that more important responses occur earlier (e.g., #1 gender, #2 cultural identity—note reemphasis in #20), that role responses are frequently culturally determined (6, 7, 8, 9, 10, 14, and 15), and that the number/percentage of culturally relevant responses suggests the strength of cultural identification. Responses descriptive of personality characteristics important to the person also occur earlier (e.g., 3, 4, 5, and 10), while others appear later (e.g., 17, 18, and 19).

4. Trainees should briefly describe (orally or in writing) their own responses that appear to have cultural origins.

5. Volunteer may share their own WAY responses with participants in discussion.

SOURCE: Kuhn and McPartland (1954).

WAY Example Answers

1. I am a woman.
2. I am a Korean American.
3. I am strong inside.
4. I am intelligent.
5. I am a good listener and speaker.
6. I am a sister.
7. I am a daughter.
8. I am a wife, niece, and granddaughter.
9. I am a writer.
10. I am prepared.
11. I am a student.
12. I am a student of life.
13. I am a lover of plants.
14. I am a friend to be counted on.
15. I am a good daughter.
16. I am all these things and more I have yet to discover.
17. I am caring.
18. I am a person with a big mouth who talks too much.
19. I am a person with a large self-conscious.
20. I am someone with a cool middle name, which I am proud of (Jeong).

SOURCE: Dana, R.H. (2005) *Multicultural assessment principles, applications, and examples.* Mahwah, NJ: Lawrence Erlbaum and Associates.

Way

There are 20 numbered blanks on the page below. Please write 20 answers to the simple question, "Who am I?" in the blanks. Just give 20 different answers to the question. Answer as if you were giving the answers to yourself, not to somebody else. Write the answers in the order that they occur to you. Don't worry about the logic or "importance." Go fairly fast, for time is limited.

1.

2.

3.

4.

5.

6.

7.

8.

9.

10.

11.

12.

13.

14.

15.

16.

17.

18.

19.

20.

Module 2 Handout 2 (Slide 16)

Scale to Assess World Views (SAWV)

1. This scale is self-administered and designed to be self-scored by trainees with assistance, if needed, from the trainer.

2. Trainers should have read at least the two major references (e.g., Ibrahim & Kahn, 1987; Sodowsky, Kwan, & Pannu, 1994) and are also encouraged to examine Ibrahim (1985) and Ibrahim and Owen (1994) as aids for structuring the discussion.

Scale to Assess World Views (SAWV)*

This is a survey to assess some of your attitudes toward the world and people. Of course, there are no right or wrong answers. The best answer is what you feel is true of yourself.

Circle the answer that best describes your attitude.					
Please respond to each of the questions according to the following scheme:					
	Strongly Disagree	Disagree	Undecided	Agree	Strongly Agree
1. People are a combination of good and evil.	1	2	3	4	5
2. There will always be a great lack of understanding between the older and younger generation.	1	2	3	4	5
3. Technology has advanced to the point where natural disasters cannot hurt people.	1	2	3	4	5
4. Nowadays, a person has to live pretty much for today and let tomorrow take care of itself.	1	2	3	4	5
5. No weakness or difficulty can hold us back if we have enough willpower.	1	2	3	4	5
6. Human nature being what it is, there will always be war and conflict.	1	2	3	4	5
7. Women who want to remove the word *obey* from the marriage service do not understand what it means to be a wife.	1	2	3	4	5
8. Sometimes I wonder how the earlier generations survived the elements of nature.	1	2	3	4	5
9. The past is no more, the future may never be, and the present is all we can be certain of.	1	2	3	4	5
10. Commitment to a meaningful career is a very important part of a person's life.	1	2	3	4	5
11. Beneath the polite and smiling surface of human nature is a bottomless pit of evil.	1	2	3	4	5
12. People would be a lot better off if they could live far away from other people and never have anything to do with them.	1	2	3	4	5
13. I believe life is easier in the cities where one has access to all modern amenities.	1	2	3	4	5
14. Since the present is so unbearable, the future is unknown; I take comfort in the past.	1	2	3	4	5

(Continued)

	Strongly Disagree	Disagree	Undecided	Agree	Strongly Agree
15. Contemplation is the highest form of human activity.	1	2	3	4	5
16. When you come right down to it, it is human nature never to do anything without an eye to one's own profit.	1	2	3	4	5
17. The reason you should not criticize others is that they will turn around and criticize you.	1	2	3	4	5
18. The forces of nature are powerful enough to destroy everything that people can build.	1	2	3	4	5
19. If I spend 14 years pursuing my education, I will have a good job in the future.	1	2	3	4	5
20. A commitment to action is more socially relevant than a commitment to any specific philosophy.	1	2	3	4	5
21. Basically, all human beings have a great potential for good.	1	2	3	4	5
22. Appreciation of others is a healthy attitude since it is the only way to have them appreciate you.	1	2	3	4	5
23. The relationship between people and nature is one of mutual coexistence.	1	2	3	4	5
24. It is important that people are involved in the present rather than being concerned with the past or the future.	1	2	3	4	5
25. The fact that I am in existence is enough for me; I do not necessarily also have to have major accomplishments in life.	1	2	3	4	5
26. Although people are intrinsically good, they have developed institutions that force them to act in opposition to their basic natures.	1	2	3	4	5
27. Letting your friends down is not so bad because you cannot accommodate everyone.	1	2	3	4	5
28. The natural world is such a beautiful place; it is a shame to destroy it with buildings, highways, and dams.	1	2	3	4	5
29. I plan for tomorrow, today is of no consequence, and the past is over with.	1	2	3	4	5

	Strongly Disagree	Disagree	Undecided	Agree	Strongly Agree
30. I prefer to relax and enjoy life as it comes.	1	2	3	4	5
31. Most people would stop and help a person whose car is disabled.	1	2	3	4	5
32. The father is the head of the household; every person in the family should follow his lead.	1	2	3	4	5
33. We are healthier when we live in harmony with our natural world.	1	2	3	4	5
34. Good memories of the past make the present bearable.	1	2	3	4	5
35. We can find happiness within ourselves.	1	2	3	4	5
36. Every person has the potential to do well.	1	2	3	4	5
37. A couple would be happiest if all their decisions were mutually agreed upon.	1	2	3	4	5
38. When natural catastrophes occur, we have to accept them.	1	2	3	4	5
39. Planning for the future allows one to accomplish all of one's goals.	1	2	3	4	5
40. I believe that feelings and human relationships are the most important things in life.	1	2	3	4	5
41. Some people will help you and others will try to hurt you.	1	2	3	4	5
42. Top management should make all the decisions; everyone in the company should follow these directions.	1	2	3	4	5
43. I feel quite powerless when faced with the forces of nature.	1	2	3	4	5
44. We need to model our lives after our parents and ancestors and focus on our glorious past.	1	2	3	4	5
45. I believe it is more important to be a good person than a successful person.	1	2	3	4	5

*Formally titled, "Scale to Assess World Views Across Cultures."

SOURCE: Ibrahim, F. A., & Owen, S. V. (1994). Factor Analytic Structure of the scale to assess world view. *Current Psychological Research and Reviews, 13*(3), 201–209.

To Score the Scale to Assess World Views (SAWV)*

1. Pull out the coding sheet.

2. Insert values you have assigned to the items above the item numbers.

3. Add the values you have assigned for each subject (e.g., HN 1) across from left to right and place your total score in the right-hand margin. Work down the list until you have inserted values for each subset, and total these across to the right-hand margin.

4. The total score obtained in each subset indicates your perspectives on each subset. The highest scores in each subscale (e.g., human nature) in Level 1, 2, or 3 indicate your perception of human nature. A split between two levels within one subscale is possible. It signifies that you value both the subsets equally.

Scale: Human Nature

HN 1 (evil)	Items: 6, 11, 16
HN 2 (good and evil)	Items: 1, 26, 41
HN 3 (good)	Items: 36, 31, 21

Scale: Human Relationships

HR 1 (lineal–hierarchical)	Items: 7, 32, 42
HR 2 (collateral–mutual)	Items: 17, 22, 37
HR 3 (individualistic)	Items: 2, 12, 27

Scale: People/Nature

PN 1 (harmony with nature)	Items: 23, 28, 33
PN 2 (subjugating and controlling nature)	Items: 3, 8, 13
PN 3 (power of nature)	Items: 18, 43, 38

Scale: Time Orientation

TO 1 (past)	Items: 14, 34, 44
TO 2 (present)	Items: 4, 9, 24
TO 3 (future)	Items: 19, 29, 39

Scale: Activity Orientation

AO 1 (being-expressive emotional)	Items: 25, 30, 45
AO 2 (being-in-becoming)	Items: 15, 35, 40
AO 3 (doing)	Items: 5, 10, 20

*Formally titled, "Scale to Assess World Views Across Cultures."

SOURCE: Ibrahim, F. A., & Owen, S. V. (1994). Factor Analytic Structure of the scale to assess world view. *Current Psychological Research and Reviews, 13*(3), 201–209.

Module 2 Handout 3 (Slide 47)

Self-Assessment of Readiness Activity: Instructions

The following questions refer to African Americans (A), American Indians (B), Asians (C), Hispanics (D), and whites (E). Please read each question and answer with 1 (*very much*), 2 (*somewhat*), and 3 (*not at all*) in the space provided under the letter representing each group.

	Group				
Question	*A*	*B*	*C*	*D*	*E*
Have you had formal training with?	___	___	___	___	___
Do you have cultural knowledge of?	___	___	___	___	___
Would you feel comfortable providing clinical services to?	___	___	___	___	___
Have you been exposed to professional views of?	___	___	___	___	___
Would you expect a favorable therapeutic relationship with?	___	___	___	___	___
Would you expect a favorable therapeutic outcome with?	___	___	___	___	___
Please add your score in each column	___	___	___	___	___
Please rank your scores by group by highest to lowest	___	___	___	___	___

SOURCE: Adapted from Paniagua, F. A. (2005). *Assessing and treating culturally diverse clients: A practical guide* (2nd ed.). Thousand Oaks, CA: Sage Publications.

Module 2 Handout 4 (Slide 76)

Culture Specific Intervention:
Evaluation of Consumers for Services

Intake Interview Summary 1 (from Geller, 1988, p. 122):

Consumer is a 25-year-old low-income white Catholic male (factory worker) with work adjustment and marital problems (married for 1 year) and a previous hospitalization 3 years earlier with similar symptomatology. Presenting symptoms include suicide preoccupation, homicidal thoughts toward wife, fear of loss of control, panic attacks, nausea, and loss of appetite. Mental status exam: tense but appropriate, oriented; denied hallucinations, delusions, ideas of reference. IQ score of 85. Average student, school dropout at 16 to work. Asthma as child, only son, oldest of four siblings. Mother perceived as dominant family member. He moved from rural area to city 1 year ago.

Instructions:

1. Please discuss some of the multicultural issues present in this case.

2. Please discuss possible barriers to consider when working with this client and strategies to overcome those barriers.

SOURCE: Geller, J. D. (1988). Racial bias in the evaluation of patients for psychotherapy. In L. Comas-Dias & E. E. H. Griffith (Eds.), *Clinical guidelines in cross-cultural mental health* (pp. 122–134). New York: John Wiley & Sons.

Culture Specific Intervention:
Evaluation of Consumers for Services

Intake Interview Summary 2 (from Geller, 1988, p. 122):

Consumer is a 25-year-old low-income African American Catholic male (factory worker) with work adjustment and marital problems (married for 1 year) and a previous hospitalization 3 years earlier with similar symptomatology. Presenting symptoms include suicide preoccupation, homicidal thoughts toward wife, fear of loss of control, panic attacks, nausea, and loss of appetite. Mental status exam: tense but appropriate, oriented; denied hallucinations, delusions, ideas of reference. I.Q. score of 85. Average student, school dropout at 16 to work. Asthma as child, only son, oldest of our siblings. Mother perceived as dominant family member. He moved from rural area to city 1 year ago.

Instructions:

1. Please discuss some of the multicultural issues present in this window.

2. Please discuss possible barriers to consider when working with this client and strategies to overcome those barriers.

SOURCE: Geller, J. D. (1988). Racial bias in the evaluation of patients for psychotherapy. In L. Comas-Dias & E. E. H. Griffith (Eds.), *Clinical guidelines in cross-cultural mental health* (pp. 122–134). New York: John Wiley & Sons.

Culture Specific Intervention:
Evaluation of Consumers for Services

Intake Interview Summary 3 (from Geller, 1988, p. 122)

Consumer is a 25-year-old low-income Latino Catholic male (factory worker) with work adjustment and marital problems (married for 1 year) and a previous hospitalization 3 years earlier with similar symptomatology. Presenting symptoms include suicide preoccupation, homicidal thoughts toward wife, fear of loss of control, panic attacks, nausea, and loss of appetite. Mental status exam: tense but appropriate, oriented; denied hallucinations, delusions, ideas of reference. I.Q. score of 85. Average student, school dropout at 16 to work. Asthma as child, only son, oldest of four siblings. Mother perceived as dominant family member. He moved from rural area to city 1 year ago.

Instructions:

1. Please discuss some of the multicultural issues present in this window.

2. Please discuss possible barriers to consider when working with this client and strategies to overcome those barriers.

SOURCE: Geller, J. D. (1988). Racial bias in the evaluation of patients for psychotherapy. In L. Comas-Dias & E. E. H. Griffith (Eds.), *Clinical guidelines in cross-cultural mental health* (pp. 122–134). New York: John Wiley & Sons.

Culture Specific Intervention:
Evaluation of Consumers for Services

Intake Interview Summary 4 (from Geller, 1988, p. 122):

Consumer is a 25-year-old low-income American Indian Catholic male (factory worker) with work adjustment and marital problems (married for 1 year) and a previous hospitalization 3 years earlier with similar symptomatology. Presenting symptoms include suicide preoccupation, homicidal thoughts toward wife, fear of loss of control, panic attacks, nausea, and loss of appetite. Mental status exam: tense but appropriate, oriented; denied hallucinations, delusions, ideas of reference. I.Q. score of 85. Average student, school dropout at 16 to work. Asthma as child, only son, oldest of four siblings. Mother perceived as dominant family member. He moved from rural area to city 1 year ago.

Instructions:

1. Please discuss some of the multicultural issues present in this window.

2. Please discuss possible barriers to consider when working with this client and strategies to overcome those barriers.

SOURCE: Geller, J. D. (1988). Racial bias in the evaluation of patients for psychotherapy. In L. Comas-Dias & E. E. H. Griffith (Eds.), *Clinical guidelines in cross-cultural mental health* (pp. 122–134). New York: John Wiley & Sons.

Culture Specific Intervention:
Evaluation of Consumers for Services

Intake Interview Summary 5 (from Geller, 1988, p. 122):

Consumer is a 25-year-old low-income Korean American Catholic male (factory worker) with work adjustment and marital problems (married for 1 year) and a previous hospitalization 3 years earlier with similar symptomatology. Presenting symptoms include suicide preoccupation, homicidal thoughts toward wife, fear of loss of control, panic attacks, nausea, and loss of appetite. Mental status exam: tense but appropriate, oriented; denied hallucinations, delusions, ideas of reference. IQ score of 85. Average student, school dropout at 16 to work. Asthma as child, only son, oldest of four siblings. Mother perceived as dominant family member. He moved from rural area to city 1 year ago.

Instructions:

1. Please discuss some of the multicultural issues present in this window.

2. Please discuss possible barriers to consider when working with this client and strategies to overcome those barriers.

SOURCE: Geller, J. D. (1988). Racial bias in the evaluation of patients for psychotherapy. In L. Comas-Dias & E. E. H. Griffith (Eds.), *Clinical guidelines in cross-cultural mental health* (pp. 122–134). New York: John Wiley & Sons.

MODULE 2 HANDOUT 4 (SLIDE 76) (CONTINUED)

References

Arendt, H. (1970). *On violence.* New York: Harcourt, Brace, & World.

Atkinson, D. R., Morten, G., & Sue, D. W. (1998). *Counseling American minorities: A cross-cultural perspective* (5th ed.). New York: McGraw-Hill.

Bates, S. C., Beauvais, F., & Trimble, J. E. (1997). American Indian adolescent involvement and ethnic identification. *Substance Use & Misuse, 32*(14), 2013–2031.

Bernal, G., Trimble, J. E., Burlew, A. K., & Leong, F. T. L. (2003). *Handbook of racial & ethnic psychology.* Thousand Oaks, CA: Sage.

Cardemil, E. V., & Battle, C. L. (2003). Guess who's coming to therapy? Getting comfortable with conversations about race and ethnicity in therapy. *Professional Psychology: Research and Practice, 37,* 66–74.

Casas, J. M., & Pytluk, S. D. (1995). Hispanic identity development. In J. G. Ponterotto, J. M. Casas, L. A. Suzuki, & C. M. Alexander (Eds.), *Handbook of multicultural counseling* (pp. 155–180). Thousand Oaks, CA: Sage.

Comas-Diaz, L., Lykes, M. B., & Alarcon, R. D. (1998). Ethnic conflict and the psychology of liberation in Guatemala, Peru, and Puerto Rico. *American Psychologist, 53,* 778–792.

Cross, W. (1991). *Shades of black: Diversity in African American identity.* Philadelphia: Temple University Press.

Cross, W. E. (1995). The psychology of nigrecence: Revising the Cross model. In J. G. Ponterotto, J. M. Casas, L. A. Suzuki, & C. M. Alexander (Eds.), *Handbook of multicultural counseling* (pp. 93–122). Thousand Oaks, CA: Sage.

Cross, W. E., & Vandiver, B. J. (2001). Nigrescence theory and measurement: Introducing the Cross Racial Identity Scale (CRIS). In J. G. Ponterotto, J. M. Casas, L.A. Suzuki, & C. M. Alexander (Eds.), *Handbook of multicultural counseling* (2nd ed., pp. 371–393). Thousand Oaks, CA: Sage.

Cuéller, I., Arnold, B., & Maldonado, R. (1995). Acculturation Rating Scale for Mexican Americans-II: A revision of the original ARSMA scale. *Hispanic Journal of Behavioral Sciences, 17*(3), 275–304.

Cullen, C. (1927). *On these I stand: An anthology of the best poems.* New York: Harper.

Dana, R. H. (1993). *Multicultural assessment perspectives for professional psychology.* Boston: Allyn & Bacon.

Dana, R. H. (1998). *Understanding cultural identity in intervention and assessment.* Thousand Oaks, CA: Sage.

Dana, R. H. (2005). *Multicultural assessment principles, applications, and examples.* Mahwah, NJ: Erlbaum.

Dobbins, J. E., & Skillings, J. H. (2000). Racism as a clinical syndrome. *American Journal of Orthopsychiatry, 70,* 14–27.

Essed, P. (1990). *Everyday racism: Reports from women of two cultures.* Claremont, CA: Hunter House.

Freire, P. (1970). *The pedagogy of the oppressed.* New York: Seabury Press.

Geller, J. D. (1988). Racial bias in the evaluation of patients for psychotherapy. In L. Comas-Diaz & E. E. H. Griffith (Eds.), *Clinical guidelines in cross-cultural mental health* (pp. 112–134). New York: John Wiley.

Hansen, N. D., Rendazzo, K. V., Schawartz, A., Marshall, M., Kalis, D., Frazier, R., et al. (2006). Do we practice what we preach? An exploratory survey of multicultural psychotherapy competencies. *Professional Psychology: Research and Practice, 37,* 66–74.

Harrell, S. P. (2000). A multidimensional conceptualization of racism-related stress: Implications for the well being of people of color. *American Journal of Orthopsychiatry, 70,* 42–57.

Helms, J. E., & Carter, R. T. (1990). Development of the White Racial Identity Inventory. In J. E. Helms (Ed.), *Black and white racial identity: Theory, research, and practice* (pp. 67–80). Westport, CT: Greenwood.

Ibrahim, F. A. (1985). Effective cross-cultural counseling and psychotherapy: A framework. *The Counseling Psychologist, 14,* 625–638.

Ibrahim, F. A., & Kahn, H. (1987). Assessment of world views. *Psychological Reports, 60,* 163–176.

Ibrahim, F. A., & Owen, S. V. (1994). Factor analytic structure of the scale to assess world view. *Current Psychological Research and Reviews, 13*(3), 201–209.

Ibrahim, F. A., Roysircar-Sodowsky, G., & Ohnishi, H. (2001). Worldview: Recent developments and needed directions. In J. G. Ponterotto, J. M. Casas, L. S. Suzuki, & C. M. Alexander (Eds.), *Handbook of multicultural counseling* (pp. 425–456).Thousand Oaks: Sage.

Johnson, A. G. (2001). *Privilege, power and difference.* Mountain View, CA: Mayfield.

Jones, J. M. (1997). *Prejudice and racism* (2nd ed.). New York: McGraw-Hill.

Kluckhohn, F. R., & Strodtbeck, F. L. (1961). *Variations in value orientations.* Evanston, IL: Row & Peterson.

La Roche, M. F., & Maxie, A. (2003). Ten considerations in addressing cultural differences in psychotherapy. *Professional Psychology: Research and Practice, 34,* 180–186.

Marger, M. (2005). *Social inequality* (3rd ed.). New York: McGraw-Hill.

Maxie, A. C., Arnold, D. H., & Stephenson, M. (2006). Do therapists address ethnic and racial differences in cross-cultural psychotherapy? *Psychotherapy: Theory, Research, Practice, Training, 43,* 85–98.

McIntosh, P. (1989, July/August). White privilege: Unpacking the invisible knapsack. *Peace and Freedom,* 10–12.

McIntosh, P. (2000). White privilege and male privilege: A personal account of coming to see correspondences through work in women's studies. In T. E. Ore (Ed.), *The social construction of differences in inequality: Race, class, gender, and sexuality* (pp. 475–485). Mountain View, CA: Mayfield.

Neville, H. A., Worthington, R. L., & Spanierman, L. B. (2001). Race, power, and multicultural counseling psychology: Understanding white privilege and color-blind racial attitudes. In J. G. Ponterotto, J. M. Casas, L. A. Suzuki, & C. M. Alexander (Eds.), *Handbook of multicultural counseling* (2nd ed., pp. 257–288). Thousand Oaks, CA: Sage.

Pinderhughes, E. (1989). *Understanding race, ethnicity, and power: The key to efficacy in clinical practice.* New York: Free Press.

Ponterotto, J. G., Casas, J. M., Suzuki, L. A., & Alexander, C. M. (2001). *Handbook of multicultural counseling* (2nd ed.). Thousand Oaks, CA: Sage.

Ridley, C. R., & Lingle, D. W. (1996). Clinical empathy in multicultural counseling: A multidimensional process model. In P. B. Pedersen, J. G. Draguns, W. J. Lonner, & J. E. Trimble (Eds.), *Counseling across cultures* (4th ed., pp. 21–46). Thousand Oaks, CA: Sage.

Ruiz, A. S. (1990). Ethnic identity: Crisis and resolution. *Journal of Multicultural Counseling and Development, 18,* 29–40.

Sears, J. T., & Williams, W. L. (1997). *Overcoming heterosexism and homophobia: Strategies that work.* New York: Columbia University Press.

Sodowsky, G. R., Kwan, K. K., & Pannu, R. (1995). Ethnic identity of Asians, in the United States. In J. G. Ponterotto, J. M. Casas, L. A. Suzuki, & C. M. Alexander (Eds.), *Handbook of multicultural counseling* (pp. 155–180). Thousand Oaks, CA: Sage.

Spohn, C. (2000). Thirty years of sentencing reform: The quest for racially neutral sentencing process. *Criminal Justice, 3,* 427–501.

Sue, D. W., & Sue, D. (2003). *Counseling the culturally diverse: Theory and practice* (4th ed.). New York: Houghton Mifflin.

Suinn, R. M., Ahuna, C., & Kloo, G. (1992). The Suinn-Lew Asian Self-Identity Acculturation Scale: Concurrent and factorial validation. *Educational and Psychological Measurement, 52,* 1041–1046.

Trimble, J. E., Helms, J. E., & Root, M. P. P. (2003). Social and psychological perspectives on ethnic and racial identity. In G. Bernal, J. E., Trimble, A. K. Burlew, & F. T. Leong (Eds.), *Handbook of racial & ethnic minority psychology* (pp. 239–275). Thousand Oaks, CA: Sage.

U.S. Department of Health and Human Services. (2001). *Mental health: Culture, race and ethnicity: A supplement to mental health: A report of the Surgeon General—Executive summary.* Rockville, MD: Author.

Utsey, S. O., Bolden, M. A., & Brown, A. S. (2001). Visions of revolution from the spirit of Franz Fanon. A psychology of liberation for counseling African Americans confronting societal racism and oppression. In J. G. Ponterotto, J. M. Casas, L. A. Suzuki, & C. M. Alexander (Eds.), *Handbook of multicultural counseling* (2nd ed., pp. 311–336). Thousand Oaks, CA: Sage.

Utsey, S. O., Gernat, C. A., & Hammar, L. (2005). Examining white counselor trainees' reactions to racial issues in counseling and supervision dyads. *The Counseling Psychologist, 33,* 449–478.

Young, I. M. (2001). Five faces of oppression. In M. Adams, W. J. Blumenfeld, R. Casteñeda, H. W. Hackman, M. L. Peters, & X. Zuñiga (Eds.), *Reading for diversity and social justice* (pp. 35–49). New York: Routledge.

Zimmerman, M. A., Ramirez-Valles, J., Washienki, K. M., Walter, B., & Dyer, S. (1996). The development of a measure of enculturation for Native American youth. *American Journal of Community Psychology, 24*(2), 295–310.

Module **3**

SENSITIVITY AND RESPONSIVENESS TO CONSUMERS

Slides

**Module 3
Sensitivity and Responsiveness
to Consumers**

CBMCS

Acknowledgments

Richard H. Dana, Regional Research Institute for
Human Services, Portland State University
Glenn C. Gamst, University of La Verne
Aghop Der-Karabetian, University of La Verne

With Contributions From
Leticia Arellano-Morales, University of La Verne
Marya Endriga, California State University, Sacramento
Robbin Huff-Musgrove, San Bernardino County Department of
Behavioral Health
Gloria Morrow, Private Practice

With Generous Support From
California Department of Mental Health–Office of
Multicultural Services
Eli Lilly Foundation
California Mental Health Directors Association
California Institute of Mental Health
University of La Verne, La Verne, CA

CBMCS

Introductions

CBMCS

Module 3 Overview

1. Highlights
2. Sensitivity and Responsiveness Defined
3. Communication Styles
4. Stereotyping
5. Racism and Mental Health
6. Racism Effects on Consumers
7. Use of Active Engagement to Ameliorate Effects of Racism
8. Guiding Principles for Sensitive and Responsive Mental Health Practice
9. Clinical Implications

CBMCS

Goals and Objectives

- To improve sensitivity to the experiences and worldview of consumers
- To improve sensitivity and responsiveness to the effects of racism, oppression, and discrimination on consumers of mental health services
- To improve sensitivity to the impact of provider and consumer social values and communication styles

CBMCS

Goals and Objectives (continued)

- To improve sensitivity to the importance of consumer advocacy
- To increase sensitivity for clinical practice implications
- To critique traditional theories and consider new ones such as recovery models and evidence based practices

(Anthony, 2000)

CBMCS

Cultural Competency Review

CBMCS

Modules 1 and 2 Highlights

1. What is culture?
2. How does racial identity affect treatment?
3. How does acculturation affect treatment?
4. What are different types of racism?
5. How do power differentials affect treatment?

CBMCS

Sensitivity and Responsiveness to Consumers

CBMCS

Sensitivity and Responsiveness: Definition

- Sensitivity refers to the provider's ability to understand consumers' experiences of racism, oppression, and discrimination.
- Provider responsiveness affects the experience of being a mental health consumer and his or her level of functioning.

CBMCS

Sensitivity and Responsiveness: Communication Styles

- Sensitivity refers to providers' acknowledgment and understanding that they may hold different social values and communication styles than the consumers they serve.
- Responsiveness to these differences may improve the quality of the therapeutic relationship.

CBMCS

Cultural-Contextual Influences on Communications

- Cultural context: Race, language, individualism, collectivism
- Physical environment: Location of internship (clinic, classroom, office). Linear thinking styles are commonly embedded in therapeutic processes
- Social relationship: Consumer/provider, student/teacher, wife/husband
- Perceptual environment: Interlocutors' attitudes, motives, cognitive styles, personality traits
- High-context individuals focus on the nonverbal aspects of the message
- Low-context individuals attend more closely to the verbal message

(Neuliep, 2006)

CBMCS

Communication Styles

- Direct-indirect: Speakers' willingness to disclose intentions in verbal communications
- Elaborate-succinct: Volume and quantity of talk
- Personal-contextual: Use of generic/specific personal pronoun, informality-formality
- Instrumental-affective: Goal/outcome oriented vs. collaborative/process oriented talk

(Neuliep, 2006)

Direct-Indirect Styles

- Persons using direct communication styles prefer precise, candid statements (common with individualistic cultures). Indirect styles make use of ambiguity, vagueness, and hints (common in collectivistic cultures).
- A: Let's talk about how you feel about your parents?
- B: OK.
- A: Do you sometimes get angry with them?
- B: I'm not sure.

(Neuliep, 2006)

Elaborate-Succinct Styles

- Elaborate communication styles tend to embellish language with metaphors, similes, and adjectives (common in some Arab, Middle Eastern, and African American cultures). Succinct styles value the use of concise talk and silence (e.g., cultures of Japan, China, and Native Americans).
- A: I bet you nearly blew a fuse when she told you who she was seeing.
- B: Yes, I was troubled.
- A: I would have been madder than a nest of hornets.
- B: I was quite upset.

(Neuliep, 2006)

Personal-Contextual Styles

- Personal communication styles rely on first-person pronouns and informality (and are used widely in the United States). Rank and status are often ignored with this style, and instead, a generic you is involved. Contextual styles emphasize one's role, status, and identity and are found in many Asian languages as well as French, German and Spanish.
- A: I was really stressed by that final exam. I hated it.
- B: Yes, Ms. Jones, it was difficult.
- A: I prefer take-home exams where I can concentrate in the comfort of my home.
- B: Yes, that would be nice.

(Neuliep, 2006)

Instrumental-Affective Styles

- Instrumental communication styles are pragmatic, persuasive, and outcome oriented. Are often used by white American males. Instrumental styles place the comprehension burden on the communication recipient. Affective styles are more process oriented and less focused on outcome. Affective speakers monitor their audience. Many Asian cultures (Japanese, Chinese) adopt an affective communication style.
- A: Mr. Chen, welcome to my office. I am eager to get started discussing your concerns.
- B: Good afternoon. You have a very lovely office. Is that a picture of your family on your desk?
- A: Yes, it is. Now about those concerns. . . .
- B: You must be very proud of your family.

(Neuliep, 2006)

Cultural Influences
on Communication:
Nonverbal Behavior

- Nonverbal behavior is influenced by culture, age, gender, personal idiosyncrasies, and the situation.
- 65%–90% of a message's meaning is communicated nonverbally.
- Sensitive and responsive providers work to familiarize themselves with nonverbal signals common to cultural groups that they serve.

(Birdwhistell, 1970; Knapp & Hall, 2006; Neuliep, 2006)

Nonverbal Communication Channels

- <u>Kinesics:</u> Deals with body, hand, arm and leg movement, gestures, facial expression, eye gaze, stance, and posture. Kinesic behaviors vary across cultures (e.g., bowing is customary greeting for Koreans and other Asian cultures).
- <u>Paralanguage:</u> Includes voice qualities (e.g., pitch, rhythm, tempo, articulation, resonance), vocalization (e.g., laughing, crying, sighing, belching, swallowing, throat clearing, snoring), and filled pauses (e.g., uh, ah, um), and silence. Paralanguage varies across cultures, too (e.g., clicking sounds of South Africa's Zulu and Xhosa languages).
- <u>Proxemics:</u> Refers to the perception and use of space, including personal space. Cultures with high-density populations value personal space.
- <u>Haptics:</u> Refers to the use of touch. Haptic communication varies across cultures. South and Central American and Southern European cultures engage in contact/touching more than Asian cultures.
- <u>Olfactics:</u> Refers to our sense of smell. Americans are the biggest consumers of fragrances (2 million lbs./yr).
- <u>Chronemics:</u> Refers to the perception of time. Monochronic time-oriented cultures (e.g., United States, Germany, Scandinavia, Canada, France) emphasize schedules and time units. Polychronic time-oriented cultures (e.g., Southern Europe, Latin America, and most African and Middle Eastern countries) see time as less tangible, focus on tasks and process, not schedules.

(Neuliep, 2006)

Sensitivity and Responsiveness: Stereotyping

- Providers need to recognize the ethnic/racial/cultural stereotypes they might have in order to minimize any negative impact when providing mental health services.

(Ponterotto, Utsey, & Pedersen, 2006)

The Gun-Toting White Male

© Louie Psihoyos/Corbis.

Prison Inmate vs. Retiree

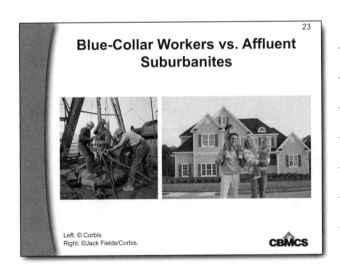

Top: © Sophie Elbaz/Sygma/Corbis.
Bottom: © Catherine Karnow/Corbis.

CBMCS

Blue-Collar Workers vs. Affluent Suburbanites

Left: © Corbis.
Right: ©Jack Fields/Corbis.

CBMCS

Activity

- Large group sharing
- Please list some stereotypes about Americans

CBMCS

Stereotypes About U.S. Americans by Spaniards Between 15 and 21 Who Have Never Been to the U.S. or Had American Friends

- Physical appearance and dress:
  - Most Americans are very tall with blue eyes and blond hair.
  - American women are either unusually fat or unusually thin, never of normal build.
  - The typical American "native dress" is jeans, cowboy boots, and a cowboy hat.

U.S. Stereotypes (continued)

- Work and leisure:
  - Americans spend almost all day at work; they have very little free time.
  - The first two things an American wants to discuss are salary and age.
- Communication and social interaction:
  - Americans speak very quickly and very loudly. They use their hands a lot, often gesturing in an exaggerated way when they talk. Their strange intonation makes their speech sound like singing.

U.S. Stereotypes (continued)

- Communication and social interaction:
  - The typical American is very rude, often putting his feet on a desk or table and frequently belching in public. He yawns a lot, never trying to hide it. In international affairs as in personal life, Americans do whatever they want and don't care what other people think.
- Home life:
  - Americans divorce repeatedly and have very complicated private lives.
  - American cities are so dangerous that a person has a good chance of being killed in the street; therefore, American men either know kung-fu or carry a gun.

U.S. Stereotypes (continued)

- Food:
  - Americans eat almost nothing but hamburgers, hot dogs, popcorn, and Coke.
  - American men are always drinking beer, even at breakfast.

Source: www.serve.com/shea/streotyp.htm

CBMCS

Who Is an American Indian?

Source: Smith, J.-Q-T.S., (2007). Who is An American Indian? In *Unlimited boundaries: Dichotomy of place in contemporary Native American art.* (Available from Albuquerque Museum of Art and History, 200 Mountain Road, NW, Albuquerque, NM 87104)

CBMCS

Who Is an American Indian? (continued)

1. Given name: Jennifer
   Ethnic identity: Russian Jewish, American and Austrian
2. Given name: Mojo
   Ethnic identity: Roma, Romanian and Hungarian
3. Given name: LaTanya
   Ethnic identity: African American and French Canadian
4. Given name: Henry
   Ethnic identity: Mexican and Mayan
5. Given name: Karen
   Ethnic identity: Navajo (Diné)
6. Given name: Deidre
   Ethnic identity: Navajo
7. Given name: Clarissa
   Ethnic identity: Fillipino
8. Given name: Paul
   Ethnic identity: Italian and Irish
9. Given name: Alayna
   Ethnic identity: Diné (Navajo)
10. Given name: Raven
    Ethnic identity: Navajo and Chicano
11. Given name: Nathaniel
    Ethnic identity: Japanese and Italian
12. Given name: Carm
    Ethnic identity: Apache, Tarahumara and Mexican
13. Given name: Neal
    Ethnic identity: Flathead Salish, Cree and Métis
14. Given name: Yamel
    Ethnic identity: Mexican and Mayan
15. Given name: Fred
    Ethnic identity: Scandinavian, Chickasaw and Choctaw
16. Given name: Celina
    Ethnic identity: Spanish and Irish
17. Given name: Ken
    Ethnic identity: African American and Choctaw
18. Given name: Masami
    Ethnic identity: Japanese
19. Given name: Jordan
    Ethnic identity: Grand Portage Chippewa and European
20. Given name: Miranda
    Ethnic identity: Haitian American and Anglo

Source: Smith, J.-Q-T.S., (2007). Who is An American Indian? In *Unlimited boundaries: Dichotomy of place in contemporary Native American art.* (Available from Albuquerque Museum of Art and History, 200 Mountain Road, NW, Albuquerque, NM 87104)

CBMCS

Racism and Mental Health

CBMCS

Racism

- A system of dominance, power, and privilege based on racial-group designations that is created and accepted by the dominant group.
- Rooted in the historical oppression of a group defined or perceived by dominant-group members as inferior, deviant, or undesirable.

(Harrell, 2000)

CBMCS

Racism and Mental Health: Barriers to Service

- Provider's perspective:
  - Failure to acknowledge the long history of racism and its impact on mental health services for people of color.
  - Failure to acknowledge the pervasiveness of racism in the lives of consumers.
  - Failure to acknowledge how individual, institutional, cultural racism has influenced conventional treatment modalities, diagnoses, and assessment.

CBMCS

Racism and Mental Health: Barriers to Service (continued)

- Consumer's perspective:
  - Failure to trust the mental health system.
- Agency's perspective:
  - Failure to acknowledge that racism is also an institutional/ systemic problem and that the agency may also perpetuate racism.
  - Failure to acknowledge that changes must be made at every level of the agency.

(Ponterotto, Utsey, & Pedersen, 2006; also see Sue et al., 2007, for a discussion of racial microaggressions)

CBMCS

Dialogue

- Form small groups and select a recorder and reporter.
- Given the definition of racism presented, please share a personal example of racism that you have witnessed or heard of occurring in a mental health setting.
- Please share the impact it had on the consumer and its impact on you.

CBMCS

Racism Effects on Consumers

CBMCS

Racism Effects on Consumers: Racism as a Stressor

- Racism-related life events (e.g., racial slur)
- Vicarious racism experiences (e.g., racial profiling)
- Daily racial microstressors (e.g., being ignored in line)
- Chronic contextual distress (e.g., employment and housing barriers)
- Collective experiences (e.g., Confederate flag)
- Transgenerational trauma (e.g., Japanese American internment and slavery)

(Harrell, 2000)

38

Racism Effects on Consumers: Medicalization

- Racism has dual effects: It can lead to overdiagnosis by pathologizing normal adaptive reactions to racism and to underdiagnosis by denial of treatment.
- Forms of overdiagnosis include anxiety reactions and personality disorders.
- Underdiagnosis can result in failure to recognize oppression-based trauma.

(Harrell, 2000)

39

Racism Effects on Consumers: Quality of Life

- Physical: Hypertension, cardiovascular reactivity, risk behavior (e.g., cigarette smoking)
- Psychological: Anxiety, depression, hostility, trauma-related symptoms
- Social: Social connectedness; intragroup and intergroup relations
- Functional: Academic achievement, job performance, parental functioning
- Spiritual: Loss of faith, meaninglessness, existential angst

(Harrell, 2000)

Provider Strategies for Helping Consumers Cope With Racism

When implementing a cultural formulation consider
the following interventions:

- Identify and validate racism-related stress and encourage consumers
  to talk about the events.
- Explore with consumers how context and personal characteristics
  affect their exposure to racism.
- Strengthen consumers' racial and cultural identity.
- Empower consumers by encouraging collective coping activities
  (e.g., participate in social change activities).
- Access availability of social support and role models
  for racism coping.
- Refrain from minimizing racism-related stress (i.e., questioning the
  validity of consumers' experiences or rationalizing).

(Harrell, 2000)

The Use of Active Engagement to Ameliorate the Effects of Racism and to Facilitate Recovery/Rehabilitation

---

Active Engagement: Service Delivery Social Etiquette

Service delivery social etiquette refers to credible
culture-specific styles of etiquette that show respect and
facilitate the therapeutic process.

Active Engagement: Culturally Responsive Behaviors

- Gather cultural information
- Self-disclose when culturally appropriate
- Acknowledge consumer concerns with cultural issues
- Formulate culturally consistent treatment plans/ objectives
- Balance culture-general and culture-specific assessment criteria

(Arredondo, 2002; Ridley, Mendoza, Kanitz, Angermeier, & Zenk, 1994)

Active Engagement: Consumer Coping and Recovery Strategies

- Network
- Utilize self-help groups
- Include consumers in the illness management process
- Engage in advocacy activities
- Exercise freedom of choice
- Normalize quality of life (e.g., seek employment training, education, housing)
- Utilize spiritual support
- Develop social identity beyond mental health consumer

(Anthony, 2000; California Network of Mental Health Clients, 1998, 2002)

Active Engagement: Providers and Consumers as Advocates

Providers and consumers advocate for:
- Elimination of discrimination/stigma
- Public policy change
- Case management
- Leadership system
- Staff training in recovery vision
- Funding allocations to meet consumer needs
- Access to services based on consumer preference
- Time allotment for additional support, such as home visits, providing information regarding bureaucracies
- Community outreach

(Anthony, 2000; California Network of Mental Health Clients, 1998, 2002)

**Guiding Principles for
Sensitive and Responsive
Mental Health Practice**

CBMCS

**Framework for the
Guiding Principles**

- Values
- Assumptions
- Practice

(Prilleltensky, 1997)

CBMCS

**Guiding Principles
Framework: Values**

- Caring and compassion
- Self-determination and relatedness
- Human diversity
- Collaboration and democratic participation
- Distributive justice (reallocation of resources and bargaining power)

(Prilleltensky, 1997)

CBMCS

Guiding Principles
Framework: Assumptions

49

- Knowledge for the advancement of human welfare
- Good life (provider/consumer perspective)
- Good society (provider/consumer perspective)
- Power in provider–consumer relationships

(Prilleltensky, 1997)

Guiding Principles
Framework: Practice

50

- Problem definition (e.g., personal, systemic)
- Role of the consumer (e.g., full, active participant in service process)
- Role of the provider (e.g., agents of personal-social growth and change)
- Type of intervention (e.g., symptom, holistic focus)
- Time of intervention (e.g., prevention, treatment)

(Prilleltensky, 1997)

Evaluation of
Approaches to Practice

51

<u>Conventional</u> approach focuses on personal adjustment.
<u>Empowering</u> approach enhances control consumers exercise over their lives.
<u>Postmodern</u> approach helps consumers construct their own identity and definition of their problems without constraints imposed by social roles.
<u>Emancipatory</u> <u>communitarian</u> approach fosters a balance among values of self-determination, caring and compassion, collaboration and democratic participation, human diversity, and distributive justice.

(Prilleltensky, 1997)

**Critique of Conventional
Counseling Theory**

CBMCS

**Conventional Counseling
and Psychotherapy**

- "Theories develop from individual perspectives,
  experiences, and practices, all of which are embedded
  in a particular cultural context."
- "Counseling and psychotherapy have traditionally
  been conceptualized in Western, individualistic
  terms." The assumption is that such theories based
  on this monocultural perspective are applicable to all
  populations when they are not.

(Katz, 1985, p. 617)

CBMCS

**The Components of
Standard Counseling:
Values and Assumptions**

- The individual in counseling
- Action orientation
- Status and power
- Processes (communication)
- Goals of counseling
- Protestant work ethic
- Goal orientation and progress
- Emphasis on scientific method
- Time
- Family structure

(Katz, 1985)

CBMCS

Implications for Treatment

CBMCS

Implications for Treatment

- Cultural sensitivity and responsiveness facilitate treatment and result in better outcomes for diverse clients.
- Conversely, cultural insensitivity and lack of responsiveness reduce treatment effectiveness.

CBMCS

Culturally Responsive Behavior Leads To:

- Low attrition
- High consumer satisfaction
- High consumer motivation
- High utilization
- Consumer rating of counselor as credible, empathic, and trustworthy
- Positive ratings on outcome measures

(Ridley, Mendoza, Kantiz, Angermeier, & Zenk, 1994)

CBMCS

Conclusion

58

CBMCS

Handouts

Module 3 Handout 1 (Slide 40)

Outline for Cultural Formulation

The following outline for cultural formulation is meant to supplement the multiaxial diagnostic assessment and to address difficulties that may be encountered in applying *DSM-IV* (American Psychological Association, 2000) criteria in a multicultural environment. The cultural formulation provides a systematic review of the individual's cultural background, the role of the cultural context in the expression and evaluation of symptoms and dysfunction, and the effect that cultural differences may have on the relationship between the individual and the clinician.

As indicated in the introduction to the manual (see p. vii), it is important that the clinician take into account the individual's ethnic and cultural context in the evaluation of each of the *DSM-IV* axes. In addition, the cultural formulation suggested below provides an opportunity to describe systematically the individual's cultural and social reference group and ways in which the cultural context is relevant to clinical care. The clinician may provide a narrative summary for each of the following categories:

Cultural identity of the individual. Note the individual's ethnic or cultural reference groups. For immigrants and ethnic minorities, note separately the degree of involvement with both the culture of origin and the host culture (where applicable). Also note language abilities, use, and preference (including multilingualism).

Cultural explanations of the individual's illness. The following may be identified: the predominant idioms of distress through which symptoms or the need for social support are communicated (e.g., "nerves," possessing spirits, somatic complaints, inexplicable misfortune), the meaning and perceived severity of the individual's symptoms in relation to norms of the cultural reference group, any local illness category used by the individual's family and community to identify the condition, the perceived causes or explanatory models that the individual and the reference group use to explain the illness, the current preferences for and past experiences with professional and popular sources of care.

Cultural factors related to psychosocial environment and levels of functioning. Note culturally relevant interpretations of social stressors, available social supports, and levels of functioning and disability. This would include stresses in the local social environment and the role of religion and kin networks in providing emotional, instrumental, and informational support.

Cultural elements of the relationship between the individual and the clinician. Indicate differences in culture and social status between the individual and the clinician and problems that these differences may cause in diagnosis and treatment (e.g., difficulty in communicating in the individual's first language, in eliciting symptoms or understanding their cultural significance, in negotiating an appropriate relationship or level of intimacy, in determining whether a behavior is normative or pathological).

Overall cultural assessment for diagnosis and care. The formulation concludes with a discussion of how cultural considerations specifically influence comprehensive diagnosis and care.

SOURCE: American Psychiatric Association; *DSM-IV.*

Module 3 Handout 2 (Slide 42)

Service Delivery Style: African Americans

Provider needs to demonstrate humanity/cultural knowledge to client prior to commitment/ engagement with preferred professional services.

African Americans generally need to accept the humanity and cultural understanding of a service provider prior to making any commitment or becoming engaged with proffered services. The process of sizing up and checking out has been described by microstages that include both agency/client concern and the provider's behavior as it is evaluated in treatment relationships (Gibbs, 1985) and mental health consultations (Dana, 1993, p. 42; Gibbs, 1980).

Stage

   I. *Appraisal.* Client is guarded, aloof, and superficial. Client looks for signs of genuineness, approachability, and personal authenticity from provider.

  II. *Investigative/equalization of differences.* Client tries to determine culturally relevant experience of provider by challenges to personal qualifications, values, and beliefs.

 III. *Partial identification with provider.* If satisfied with Stage II outcome, client makes overtures to personalize relationship with the provider.

  IV. *Loyalty/personal regard for provider.* If provider responds during Stage III in a flexible/ sensitive manner, client becomes less defensive and does less testing of provider intentions.

   V. *Commitment/engagement.* Treatment begins with full involvement of the client.

SOURCE: Dana, R. H. (1993). *Multicultural assessment perspectives for professional psychology.* Boston: Allyn & Bacon.

Service Delivery Style: Hispanic Americans

Cultural script for credible behavioral style (Triandis, Marin, Lisansky, & Betancourt, 1984): Simpatía (high frequencies of affiliative/affectional verbalizations). Ingredients to be faithfully attended to:

1. *Respeto.* Respect by younger for older persons, women to men, persons in authority or higher socioeconomic position

2. *Personalismo.* Preference for informal, personal, individualized attention

3. *Platicando.* Leisurely chatting to establish a warm, accepting atmosphere

4. *Confianza en confianza.* Mutual trust relationship to establish mutual generosity, intimacy, personal involvement

SOURCE: Summarized from Dana (1993, chap. 4).

Service Delivery Style: American Indians/Alaskan Natives

1. *Preassessment.* A preexisting social relationship with the client in the community will provide increased trust initially in the assessment relationship.

2. *Assessment setting.*
   a. With traditional persons, chairs may be arranged next to one another to avoid immediate eye contact.
   b. Setting may be informal with other persons.
   c. Begin with informal chitchat on topics of mutual interest and shared understandings or "common basing."
   d. This common basing always includes an identification of mutual friends and acquaintances of both provider and client within a shared social frame of reference.
   e. The client needs to be satisfied that the provider not only has knowledge of his or her tribal history and group history as an Indian person in a genocidal society but also has a personal niche as an accepted person within the larger American Indian community.
   f. In the absence of these assurances, test data may be provided that are accepted as reliable even though the data are often minimal or guarded. Use of these data can result in overinterpretation that typically includes distortion, caricature, and/or pathologization.

3. *Postassessment.* Client can anticipate a continuing social relationship with the provider, preferably within community.

NOTE: See Hornby (1983).

Service Delivery Style: Asian Americans

1. Initiate relationships using cultural knowledge of proper social etiquette.

2. Demonstrate "credibility" and "gift-giving" (Sue & Zane, 1987).
   a. Credibility of role relationships (e.g., age, gender, expertise) depends on ascribed and achieved status of provider.
   b. Symbolic gift of immediate benefit (i.e., reduced anxiety, relief from depression, recognition that experiences are shared with others) strengthens relationship to facilitate subsequent services.

3. Logical and structured approach for subsequent test administration.

NOTE: See Dana (1993, chap. 3).

Module 3 Handout 3 (Slide 53)

Critique of Counseling Theories

Common Therapies	Contributions to Multicultural Counseling	Limitations to Multicultural Counseling
Psychoanalytic therapy	Its focus on family dynamics is appropriate for working with many minority groups. The therapist's formality appeals to clients who expect professional distance. Notion of ego defense is helpful in understanding inner dynamics and dealing with environmental stresses.	Its focus on insight, intrapsychic dynamics, and long-term treatment is often not valued by clients who prefer to learn coping skills for dealing with pressing daily concerns; internal focus is often in conflict with cultural values that stress an interpersonal and environmental focus.
Adlerian therapy	Its focus on social interest, doing good for society, importance of family, goal orientation, and striving for belongingness is congruent with Eastern cultures. Focus on person-in-environment allows for cultural factors to be explored.	This approach's detailed interview about one's family background can conflict with cultures that have injunctions against disclosing family matters. Mental health providers need to make certain that the client's goals are respected.
Existential therapy	Focus is on understanding client's phenomenological world, including cultural background. This approach leads to empowerment in an oppressive society. It can help clients examine their options for change, within the context of their cultural realities.	Values of individuality, freedom, autonomy, and self-realization often conflict with cultural values of collectivism, respect for tradition, deference to authority, and interdependence. Some may be deferred by the absence of specific techniques. Others will expect more focus on surviving in the world.
Person-centered therapy	Focus is on breaking cultural barriers and facilitating open dialogue among diverse cultural populations. Main strengths are respect for client's values, active listening, welcoming of differences, nonjudgmental attitude, understanding, willingness to allow clients to determine what will be explored in sessions, and prizing of cultural pluralism.	Some of the core values of this approach may not be congruent with the client's culture. Lack of mental health provider's direction and structure are unacceptable for clients who are seeking help and immediate answers from a knowledgeable professional.
Gestalt therapy	Its focus on expressing oneself nonverbally is congruent with those cultures that look beyond words for messages. Provides many techniques in working with clients who have cultural injunctions against freely expressing feelings. Can overcome language barrier with bilingual clients. Focus on bodily expressions is a subtle way to help clients recognize their conflicts.	Clients who have been culturally conditioned to be emotionally reserved may not embrace Gestalt techniques. The quick push for expressing feelings could cause premature termination of therapy by the client. Some may not see how "being aware of present experiencing" will lead to solving their problems.

(Continued)

Critique of Counseling Theories (continued)

Common Therapies	Contributions to Multicultural Counseling	Limitations to Multicultural Counseling
Behavior therapy	Its focus on behavior rather than on feelings is compatible with many cultures. Strengths include a collaborative relationship between mental health provider and client in working toward mutually agreed-on goals, continual assessment to determine if the techniques are suited to the client's unique situation, assisting clients in learning practical skills, an educational focus, and stress on self-management strategies.	Mental health providers need to help clients assess the possible consequences of making behavioral changes. Family members may not value client's newly acquired assertive style, so clients must be taught how to cope with resistance by others.
Cognitive-behavioral therapy	The collaborative approach offers clients opportunities to express their concerns. The psychoeducational dimensions are often useful in exploring cultural conflicts and teaching new behavior. The emphasis on thinking (as opposed to identifying and expressing feelings) is likely to be acceptable to many clients. The focus on teaching and learning tends to avoid the stigma of mental illness. Clients may value active and directive stance of therapist.	Before too quickly attempting to change the beliefs and actions of clients, it is essential for the therapist to understand and respect their world. Some clients may have serious reservations about questioning their basic cultural values and beliefs. Clients could become dependent on the therapist for deciding what are appropriate ways to solve problems. There may be a fine line between being directive and promoting dependence.
Family systems therapy	Many ethnic and cultural groups place value on the role of the extended family. Many family therapists deal with extended family members and with support systems. Networking is a part of the process, which is congruent with the values of many clients. There is a greater chance for individual change if other family members are supportive. This approach offers ways of working toward the health of the family unit and the welfare of each member.	Some approaches are based on value assumptions that are not congruent with the values of clients from certain cultures. Concepts such as individuation, self-actualization, self-determination, independence, self-expression may be foreign to some clients. In some cultures, admitting problems within the family is shameful. The value of "keeping problems within the family" may make it difficult to explore conflicts openly.
Reality therapy	Focus is on members' making own evaluation of behavior (including how they respond to their culture). Through personal assessment they can determine the degree to which their needs and wants are being satisfied. They can find a balance between retaining their own ethnic identity and integrating some of the values and practices of the dominant society.	This approach stresses taking charge of one's own life, yet some clients hope to change their external environment. Mental health professionals need to appreciate the role of discrimination and racism and help clients deal with social and political realities.

SOURCE: Corey, G. (2001). *Theory and practice of counseling and psychotherapy* (6th ed.). Pacific Grove, CA: Brooks/Cole Publishing Company.

References

Anthony, W. A. (2000). A recovery-oriented service system: Setting some system level standards. *Psychiatric Rehabilitation Journal, 24*(2), 159–168.

Arredondo, P. (2002). Counseling individuals from marginalized and underserved groups. In P. B. Pedersen, J. G. Draguns, W. J. Lonner, & J. E. Trimble (Eds.), *Counseling across cultures* (5th ed., pp. 233–250). Thousand Oaks, CA: Sage.

Birdwhistell, R. (1970). *Kinesics and context: Essays on body motion and communication.* Philadelphia: University of Pennsylvania Press.

California Network of Mental Health Clients. (1998). *Client culture trainings/focus groups project report.* Sacramento, CA: Author.

California Network of Mental Health Clients. (2002). *Our mission.* Sacramento, CA: Author. Retrieved November 13, 2007, from www.californiaclients.org/about/bylaws.cfm

Dana, R. H. (1993). *Multicultural assessment perspectives for professional psychology.* Boston: Allyn & Bacon.

Gibbs, J. T. (1980). The interpersonal orientation in mental health consultations: Toward a model of ethnic variations in counseling. *Journal of Community Psychology, 8,* 195–207.

Gibbs, J. T. (1985). Treatment relationships with black clients: Interpersonal vs. instrumental strategies. *Advances in Clinical Social Work.* Silver spring, MD: National Association of Social Workers.

Harrell, S. P. (2000). A multidimensional conceptualization of racism-related stress: Implications for the well-being of people of color. *American Journal of Orthopsychiatry, 70,* 42–57.

Hornby, R. (1983). *Competency training for human service providers.* Mission, SD: Sinte Gleska Press.

Katz, J. (1985). The sociopolitical nature of counseling. *The Counseling Psychologist, 13,* 615–624.

Knapp, M. L., & Hall, J. A. (2006). *Nonverbal communication in human interaction* (6th ed.). Belmont, CA: Wadsworth.

Neuliep, J. W. (2006). *Intercultural communication: A contextual approach* (3rd ed.). Thousand Oaks, CA: Sage.

Ponterotto, J. G., Utsey, S. O., & Pedersen, P. B. (2006). Assessments of prejudice, cultural competence, stressful effects of racism, racial and ethnic identity, and the multicultural personality. In *Preventing prejudice: A guide for counselors, educators, and parents* (pp. 243–262). Thousand Oaks, CA: Sage.

Prilleltensky, I. (1997). Values, assumptions, and practices: Assessing the moral implications of psychological discourse and action. *American Psychologist, 52,* 517–535.

Ridley, C. R., Mendoza, D. W., Kantiz, B. E., Angermeier, L., & Zenk, R. (1994). Cultural sensitivity in multicultural counseling: A perceptual schema model. *Journal of Counseling Psychology, 41,* 125–136.

Smith, J.-Q.-T.-S. (2007). Who is an American Indian? In *Unlimited boundaries: Dichotomy of place in contemporary Native American art.* (Library of Congress Control Number: 2006939378). (Available from the Albuquerque Museum of Art and History, 200 Mountain Road NW Albuquerque, NM 87104)

Sue, D. W., Capodilupo, C. M., Torino, G. C., Bucceri, J. M., Holder, A. M. B., Nadal, K. L., et al. (2007). Racial microaggressions in everyday life: Implications for clinical practice. *American Psychologist, 62,* 271–286.

Sue, D. W., & Sue, D. (2003*). Counseling the culturally diverse: Theory and practice* (4th ed.). New York: Houghton Mifflin.

Sue, S., & Zane, N. (1987). The role of culture and cultural techniques in psychotherapy. *American Psychologist, 42,* 37–45.

Triandis, H. C., Marin, G., Lisansky, J., & Betancourt, H. (1984). Simpatia as a cultural script of Hispanics. *Journal of Personality and Social Psychology, 47,* 1363–1375.

U.S. Department of Health and Human Services. (2001). *Mental health: Culture, race and ethnicity: A supplement to mental health: A report of the surgeon general—Executive summary.* Rockville, MD: Author.

Module **4**

SOCIOCULTURAL DIVERSITIES

Slides

**Module 4
Sociocultural Diversities**

CBMCS

Acknowledgments

Richard H. Dana, Regional Research Institute for
Human Services, Portland State University
Glenn C. Gamst, University of La Verne
Aghop Der-Karabetian, University of La Verne

With Contributions From
Leticia Arellano-Morales, University of La Verne
Marya Endriga, California State University, Sacramento
Robbin Huff-Musgrove, San Bernardino County Department of
Behavioral Health
Gloria Morrow, Private Practice

With Generous Support From
California Department of Mental Health–Office of
Multicultural Services
Eli Lilly Foundation
California Mental Health Directors Association
California Institute of Mental Health
University of La Verne, La Verne, CA

CBMCS

Introductions

CBMCS

Module 4 Overview

- Knowledge, Awareness, and Sensitivity to:
- Sociocultural Diversities:
  - Older Adults
  - Men and Women
  - Sexual Orientation/Identities
  - Socioeconomic Status (SES)
  - Persons With Disabilities
  - Interaction Among Multiple Identities
  - Identifying Sources of Personal-Professional Bias/
    Prejudice/Discrimination

CBMCS

Goals and Objectives

- To extend the parameters of diversity beyond
  the limits of ethnic/racial populations
- To improve the delivery of socioculturally competent
  services to diverse populations
- To explore the interactions of multiple human identity
  components

CBMCS

Activity: Cultural Competency Review: Sensitivity and Responsiveness

1. What does *sensitivity* refer to in the field of cultural
   competency?
2. What are some types of *communication styles*?
3. What is *racism*?
4. What is *service delivery social etiquette*?

CBMCS

What Does *Sensitivity* Refer to in the Field of Cultural Competency?

Sensitivity refers to the provider's ability to understand consumers' experiences of racism, oppression, and discrimination.

CBMCS

What Are Some Types of *Communication Styles?*

- Direct-indirect
- Elaborate-succinct
- Personal-contextual
- Instrumental-affective

CBMCS

What Is *Racism?*

Racism is a system of dominance, power, and privilege based on racial-group designations that is created and accepted by the dominant group.

CBMCS

What Is *Service Delivery Social Etiquette?*

Service delivery social etiquette refers to credible culture-specific styles of etiquette that show respect and facilitate the therapeutic process.

CBMCS

Sociocultural Diversities

Older Adults

Gender and Culture

Sexual Orientation/Identities

Socioeconomic Status (SES)

Persons With Disabilities

CBMCS

Assessment of Sources of Bias

Consumer Population Preferences

Questionnaire

CBMCS

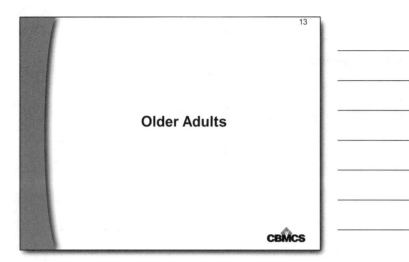

Older Adults

13

CBMCS

14

Knowledge

- The older population in the U.S. is growing.
- Those 65 and older have exceeded the growth rate of the population as a whole.
- By the year 2030, those 65 and older will constitute 20% of the population.
- Those 85 and older are the fastest growing part of the older adult population.
- Because females live longer than males, at age 65 there are only 39 older men for every 100 women.

(Sue & Sue, 2000)

CBMCS

15

Cohort Issues

- U.S. born vs. non-U.S. born
- Oldest old: 85 years +
- Middle old: 65–84 years
- Young old: 60–64 years
- Transitional adult: 50–59 years

(California Mental Health Directors Association, 2005a)

CBMCS

Awareness

"Ageism is defined as a deep and profound prejudice against the elderly which is found to some degree in all of us. . . . ageism allows the younger generations to see the older generations as different from themselves; thus they subtly cease to identify with their elders as human beings."

(Butler, 1969, pp. 11–12; see also Butler, 2002)

17

Examples of Discrimination

- Job discrimination
- Media stereotyping
- Intergenerational segregation
- Avoidance of contact
- Condescending or abusive interpersonal treatment

(Gatz & Pearson, 1988; Nelson, 2002)

18

Media Stereotypes

Copyright 2008 iStock International Inc.

Stereotypes

- Negative attitudes (stereotypes) toward older adults:
  - Rigid and not adaptable in thought processes
  - In poor health
  - Not very intelligent or alert
  - Overperception of being cognitively impaired
  - No sexual interest or belief that sexual interest is inappropriate
- These stereotypes lead to older adults feeling less valuable in society, leading to low self-esteem.

(Gatz & Pearson, 1988; Nelson, 2002)

Ageism

- Provider biases (Specific):
  - Depression is normal for older adults.
  - Psychotherapy for depression is ineffective for older adults.
  - (Positive bias) Memory lapses in the aged don't have to signify anything pathological; therefore, they do not need to be referred to a mental health professional for evaluation.
  - Substance abuse is not an issue for older adults.

(American Psychological Association, 2005; Braithwaite, 2002)

Access to Service

"One in five Americans has a diagnosable mental illness, but less than one quarter of older adults with mental illness get any type of mental health attention, let alone appropriate treatment."

(Older Women's League, 2007)

Barriers to Service

- Stigma this age group associates with mental illness
- Cultural and linguistic barriers
- Isolation of older adults
- Lack of accessibility, availability, and visibility of services
- Lack of transportation
- Lack of staff adequately trained to provide age-appropriate services
- Prevailing myths regarding inability of older adults to benefit from mental health intervention
- Lack of adequate integrated assessment of mental and physical problems
- Poor diagnosis and poor referrals
- Medicare reimbursement policy

(California Mental Health Planning Council, 2003; Hinrichsen, 2006)

Challenges Faced by Older Adults

- Economic Health:
  - Only 5% of people 65 and over live in nursing homes; this increases to 22% by age 85.
  - The rate of poverty for older adults has been decreasing from 25% in 1970 to 8.5% (65-74 yrs) to 11.5% (75+ yrs) in 1999. Rates are higher for ethnic minorities.

(Sue & Sue, 2003; U.S. Department of Health and Human Services, 1999)

Challenges Faced by Older Adults (continued)

- Economic difficulties remain for many older individuals, especially women and minority members.
- Older adult women are more likely than elderly men to be poor (16% vs. 9%).
- Poverty rates for African Americans—27% for men vs. 38% for women; for Hispanic Americans— 27% for men vs. 25% for women.

(Sue & Sue, 2003)

Challenges Faced by Older Adults (continued)

- Mental Deterioration or Incompetence:
  - A common view is that older adults are mentally incompetent. However, only a minority have dementia. Specifically, 5%–10% (over 65 yrs), 15%–20% (over 75 yrs), 25%–50% (over 85 yrs) have mild to moderate dementia.
  - Most older adults will show some decline in certain cognitive abilities, which is developmentally appropriate.

(Sue & Sue, 2003)

Caregiver Issues

- Caregiving responsibilities differ between ethnic groups:
  - 42% of Asian Americans provide care for their aging parents or other older relatives
  - 34% of Latino Americans
  - 28% of African Americans
  - 19% of White Americans
- Resources for coping across ethnic groups:
  - Religious faith
  - Family connections
  - Physicians
  - Government agencies

(Sue & Sue, 2003)

Caregiver Interventions

- Display patience and understanding
- Develop coping strategies for stress
- Educate family about neurological, memory, language problems
- Suggest practical solutions for dealing with agitation, wandering, and other safety issues
- Help family allocate caregiving responsibilities

- Improve family communication
- Address guilt feelings and other cultural factors
- Utilize community resources (e.g., Alzheimer's Association)
- Address financial and legal matters (e.g., power of attorney)
- Facilitate discussion of out-of-home care decisions

(Cox, 2005; Sue & Sue, 2003)

Challenges Faced by Older Adults (continued)

Elder Abuse and Neglect:
- Over 2 million older Americans are victims of psychological or physical abuse and neglect. This statistic is only about 20% of actual cases because of underreporting.
- Circumstances associated with abuse or neglect:
  - Pattern or history of violence in family
  - Stress and life adjustment in accommodating the older relative
  - Financial burden
  - Overcrowded quarters
  - Marital stress due to change in living arrangement

(Sue & Sue 2003; U.S. Department of Health and Human Services, 1999)

Challenges Faced by Older Adults (continued)

Substance Abuse:
- It is estimated that 17% of adults age 65 and above abuse alcohol or prescription drugs.
- Late onset alcohol and drug abuse can begin after stressors:
  - Death of family member, spouses, or friends
  - Retirement issues
  - Family conflict
  - Physical health problems
  - Financial concerns
- Older adults rarely seek treatment because of shame and discomfort in programs that treat drug addictions.

(Sue & Sue, 2003)

Challenges Faced by Older Adults (continued)

Depression and Suicide
- Males:
  - Depression increases with age.
  - Depression is associated with vascular disease, erectile dysfunction, and decreased testosterone.
  - White men older than 85 have highest suicide rate: about 6 times the national rate.
  - Older men are 7 times more likely to commit suicide than older women.
  - White men are at greater risk for suicide than nonwhite men or women.
  - Loss of health is the greatest stressor.

(American Psychological Association, 2005; Sue & Sue, 2003)

Challenges Faced by Older Adults
(continued)

- Females:
  - Higher rates of depression that decrease after age 60
  - Depression related to financial loss
- An estimated 20% of older adults in the community and as many as 50% in skilled nursing facilities suffer from depressive symptoms.
- What appears to be age related depression is depression over physical health problems and related disability.

(American Psychological Association 2005; Sue & Sue, 2003)

Challenges Faced by Older Adults
(continued)

- Sexuality and aging has been given little attention.
- Sexual interest and activities continue well into the 80s and beyond.
- In a study of 1,216 older adults avg. age 77.3, nearly 30% had sex in the last month and 67% were satisfied with their current level of activity.

(Sue & Sue, 2003)

Best Practices for Older Adults

1. Obtain specific knowledge and skills
2. Evaluate your attitude and beliefs
3. Obtain knowledge about legal and ethical issues (e.g., competency)
4. Determine reason for evaluation and social aspects of problem (e.g., recent losses, financial stressors, family issues)
5. Determine consumer's view of the problem based on beliefs, stage of life, SES, and ethnicity

(California Mental Health Directors Association, 2005b; Hill, Thorn, & Packard, 2000; Sue & Sue, 2003)

Best Practices for
Older Adults (continued)

6. Identify medical conditions and prescriptions and over-the-counter medication usage to rule out drug interactions.
7. Presume competence unless the contrary is obvious.
8. Adjust the pace of therapy to accommodate cognitive slowing.
9. Provide information appropriate for cognitive level of functioning, use alternative methods when necessary (e.g., videotape, visual aids).
10. Involve consumer in decision making as much as possible; determine if legally recognized people should be involved.
11. Use multiple assessments and collateral information.
12. Determine role of caregiver and provide education.

(California Mental Health Directors Association, 2005b; Hill,
Thorn, & Packard, 2000; Sue & Sue, 2003)

Best Practices for
Older Adults (continued)

13. Help couples negotiate time spent alone and together, especially after retirement.
14. Help individuals who are alone establish support systems.
15. Assist in developing a sense of life fulfillment by reviewing positive aspects of life experience.
16. Assist in interpreting the effects of culture, ethnic group membership, gender, and sexual orientation on consumer's life.
17. Help with end-of-life planning (e.g., deciding how important objects will be distributed and cared for).

(California Mental Health Directors Association, 2005b;
Hill, Thorn, & Packard, 2000; Sue & Sue, 2003)

Gender and Culture

"And ain't I a woman? Look at me! Look at my arm! I have ploughed and planted, and gathered into barns, and no man could head me! And ain't I a woman? I could work as much and eat as much as a man—when I could get it—and bear the lash as well! And ain't I a woman? I have borne thirteen children, and seen most all sold off to slavery, and when I cried out with my mother's grief, none but Jesus heard me! And ain't I a woman?"

—Sojourner Truth, 1851

(Internet Modern History Sourcebook, 1997)

37

Gender and Culture Overview

- Key terms
- The relationship between culture and gender role conflict in the four major ethnic groups
- Culture as a foundation in assessment and treatment of mental health and adjustment issues associated with gender role conflict

(Canales, 2000)

38

Knowledge: Key Terms

- Anatomical sex (at birth): male, female, and hermaphrodites/intersexual
  - Male: An individual who anatomically has an unambiguous penis and reproductive system.
  - Female: An individual who anatomically has an unambiguous vagina and reproductive system.
  - Intersex: An individual who has ambiguous genitalia or reproductive system.

(Sax, 2002)

39

Knowledge: Key Terms (continued)

- Transgendered: Individuals whose cognitive sense of gender is inconsistent with their anatomical sex/gender.
- Transgendered consumers may be more vulnerable to suicide attempts, substance abuse, and emotional distress when they are unable to have a sex change due to chronic mental illness.

Knowledge: Key Terms (continued)

- Gender identity:
  - Internalized acceptance of the socially defined ways of being male or female
- Gender role:
  - Behaviors, expectations, and role sets determined by social, historical, and cultural contexts

(Sax, 2002)

Knowledge: Key Terms (continued)

- Gender role:
  - Femininity
  - Masculinity
- Gender role conflict: a set of values, attitudes, or behaviors learned during socialization that causes negative psychological effects on a person or on other people

(Canales, 2000)

Awareness

- There is a dynamic interaction between gender roles and other factors that impact service delivery.
- Culturally competent delivery of mental health services requires an incorporation of the multiple factors that interact with gender.

43

Interaction of Gender Roles With Other Factors Affecting Service Delivery

- Acculturation
- Religion/spirituality
- Ethnic/racial identity
- Socioeconomic status
- Age
- Education
- Disability
- Other

CBMCS

44

Types of Gender Role Conflict

- Acculturation, ethnic identity, and immigrant status have an impact on the type and degree of gender role conflict.
- Stress of trying to abide by the gender role norms of a particular racial/ethnic minority group.

(Canales, 2000)

CBMCS

45

Impact of Gender Role Issues on Treatment

Consider the following gender role issues while providing services:

- Acculturation, traditional vs. nontraditional gender roles
- Collectivistic vs. individualistic
- Interdependent vs. dependent
- Perceived family dynamics

CBMCS

Impact of Gender Role Issues on Treatment (continued)

- Ethnic/culture-specific gender role expectations
- Sensitivity to consumer's gender role orientation/attitudes
- Developmental issues: gender role shift due to aging and developmental process
- Power differential
- Respecting a person's gender role identity as part of the recovery process

CBMCS

Ethnic/Culture-Specific Examples of Potential Gender Role Conflicts

	Male	Female
African American	Provider role and "cool pose" response to racism	Flexible gender role (caretaker and provider) result in role strain, exhaustion
Asian American	Conflict about high achievement for self versus family.	Confucian doctrine of "3 obediences" to father, husband, and son (vs. self needs)
Latino	Culturally acceptable emotional expression in males may be seen as weakness or femininity	Upholding values of purity, selflessness, mysticism of "La Virgen" (vs. self needs)
Native American	Traditional Native egalitarian roles result in view of male as lazy, not masculine, or not providing for wife	Traditional Native egalitarian role gives way to mainstream female subordination

(Canales, 2000)

Sexual Orientations/Identities

CBMCS

Key Terms: Sexual Orientation

"Sexual orientation is the interaction between affect and cognition such that it produces attraction, erotic desire, and ultimately philia [affinity] for members of the opposite gender, the same gender, or both."

(Alderson, 2003, p. 79)

Key Terms: Sexual Orientation (continued)

- Three sexual orientations are commonly recognized:
  - Homosexual: attraction to individuals of one's own anatomical sex
  - Heterosexual: attraction to individuals of the other anatomical sex
  - Bisexual: attraction to individuals of either anatomical sex

(American Psychological Association, 1998a; Fukuyama & Ferguson, 2000; Israel, 2003)

Key Terms: Sexual Orientation (continued)

"Persons with a homosexual orientation are most often referred to as gay (both men and women) or as lesbian (women only)."
"Research suggests that sexual orientation is shaped for most people at an early age through the complex interaction of biological, psychological, and social factors."

(American Psychological Association, 1998a)

Key Terms: Sexual Prejudice

"Sexual prejudice refers to negative attitudes based on sexual orientation, whether their target is homosexual, bisexual, or heterosexual (Herek, 2000). Thus, it can be used to characterize not only antigay and anti-bisexual hostility, but also the negative attitudes that some members of sexual minorities hold toward heterosexuals."

(Herek, 2004, p. 16)

Key Terms: Heterosexism

"Heterosexism...refers to the cultural ideology that perpetuates sexual stigma by denying and denigrating any nonheterosexual form of behavior, identity, relationship, or community."

Heterosexism:
- is inherent in cultural institutions,
- expresses and perpetuates a hierarchy of power and status (in which homosexuality is inferior to heterosexuality),
- keeps same-sex relationships and communities invisible.

(Herek, 2004, p. 16; see also Greene, 2005)

Key Terms: Homophobia

The irrational fear of individuals who are gay or lesbian or of anyone perceived to be gay or lesbian.

Key Terms: Internalized Oppression

"As one takes in the negative messages and stereotypes, there is a weakening of self-esteem, self-pride, and group pride. When the victim of the oppression is led to believe the negative views of the oppressor, this phenomenon is called *internalized oppression*. It takes the form of self-hatred, which can express itself in depression, despair, and self-abuse."

(Pharr, 1997, p. 60; see also Pharr, 1988)

CBMCS

Key Terms: Gay Identity

"Gay identity is . . . an identity status denoting those individuals who have come to identify themselves as having primarily homosexual cognition, affect, and/or behavior, and who have adopted the construct 'gay' as having personal significance to them."

(Alderson, 2003, p. 78)

CBMCS

Key Terms: Coming Out

Coming out refers to revealing a person's LGBT identity to oneself and to others. Coming out is a longitudinal, not singular, process.

CBMCS

Slide 58

Knowledge

Based on a national survey, it is estimated that about 7% of all adults regard themselves as homosexual or bisexual.

	Men	Women
Heterosexual	91%	95%
Homosexual	4%	2%
Bisexual	5%	3%

(Janus & Janus, 1993)

Slide 59

Knowledge (continued)

History of Oppression of Lesbians and Gays
- From beginning of Judeo Christian civilization through the 19th century:
  - Homosexuality was regarded as sin
  - Homosexuality was viewed as a criminal offense and in some cases punishable by death
  - Homosexuality was viewed as a curable disease that must be treated

(Connors, 2008; Westheimer & Lapater, 2005)

Slide 60

Knowledge (continued)

- 20th century:
  - Early 1900s, homosexuality deemed pathological by the American Psychiatric Association in *Diagnostic and Statistical Psychiatric Disorders*
  - 1948–1953, thinking shifts with Kinsey's research
  - 1960s and 1970s, homosexuality gaining notoriety as normal behavior
  - In 1973, the American Psychiatric Association removed homosexuality from its list of mental illness
  - In 1974, the American Bar Association approved the decriminalization of consensual adult homosexual acts

(Connors, 2008; Westheimer & Lapater, 2005)

Knowledge (continued)

- 21st century:
  - Homosexuality viewed as sin
  - Homosexuality viewed as deviant behavior
  - Gay and lesbians continue to fight for equal rights and equal protection
  - Gay and lesbians victimized by social stigmatization
  - Gay and lesbians victims of hate crimes
  - Gay and lesbians continue to experience multiple oppressions (sexual orientation, gender, race/ethnicity, age, SES, physical ability)
  - Homosexuality is one of the most difficult issues for some providers because of religious beliefs

(Connors, 2008; Westheimer & Lapater, 2005)

Knowledge (continued)

- Common beliefs and misconceptions:
  - There are only a few gay and lesbian individuals in the U.S.
  - Gay men are child molesters
  - Lesbians really want to be men, and gay men really want to be women
  - Researchers know what causes homosexuality

(Connors, 2008; Westheimer & Lapater, 2005)

Awareness

- Providers must become aware of the following:
  - Her or his attitude and knowledge of gay, lesbian, and bisexual consumers, including the need to seek consultation and to make appropriate referrals
  - One's assumptions, biases, and values regarding homosexuality and the impact on the delivery of services to gay, lesbian, and bisexual consumers
  - The impact of social stigmatization (i.e., prejudice, discrimination, and violence) on mental health
  - Within-group differences that exist within the gay/lesbian/transgendered community

(American Psychological Association, 1998b)

Awareness (continued)

- Providers must become aware of the following:
  - The impact of inaccurate or prejudicial views of homosexuality or bisexuality on the way in which the consumer's presenting problem is defined or the way in which the consumer may respond to mental health services
  - The particular circumstances and challenges facing this unique population in love relationships and family relations (i.e., parenting issues)
  - The impact of multiple identities (age, gender, race/ ethnicity, SES, and physical ability) on the mental well-being of gay, lesbian, and bisexual consumers

(American Psychological Association, 1998b)

Mental Health Issues

- Few differences exist between heterosexual, homosexual, and bisexual individuals on overall psychological functioning.
- Stress related to stigmatization increases the risk of suicide attempts, substance abuse, and emotional distress.
- Stress is related to health issues, such as
  - HIV/AIDS
  - Grief, loss, and depression due to loss of parental support and/or loss of friends and loved ones
- Stress is related to discrimination, oppression, and violence.
- Stress is related to identity development/coming-out process.

(American Psychological Association, 1998b)

Cass's Model of Gay, Lesbian, and Bisexual Sexual Identity Formation

- <u>Identity confusion:</u> Growing awareness of homosexual thoughts, feelings, or behaviors.
- <u>Identity comparison:</u> Investigation of qualities first experienced in the first stage. During data collection, contact with other gays is sought.
- <u>Identity tolerance:</u> Increased contact with gay community leading to greater empowerment.

(Cass, 1979)

Cass's Model of Gay, Lesbian, and Bisexual Sexual Identity Formation (continued)

- <u>Identity acceptance:</u> Conflict between the self and nongay others' perception is at most intense level.
- <u>Identity pride:</u> Conflict is managed through fostering a dichotomized homosexual (valued) and heterosexual (devalued) worldview. Extreme pride toward homosexual/bisexual community and intense anger toward heterosexual community.
- <u>Identity synthesis:</u> Last stage where movement most likely occurs when individuals experience positive reactions from heterosexual community.

(Cass, 1979)

CBMCS

Ecological Model of Gay Male Identity

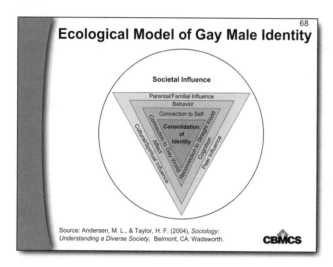

Source: Andersen, M. L., & Taylor, H. F. (2004), *Sociology: Understanding a Diverse Society.* Belmont, CA: Wadsworth.

CBMCS

Treatment Considerations With Gay, Lesbian, and Bisexual Consumers

Professional ethics dictate that providers with strong religious and/or personal beliefs that do not accept the viability of a nonheterosexual orientation should not treat this population.

- The coming-out process may differ across various consumer groups (e.g., older adults, disabled individuals, etc.).
- The consequences for multicultural community coming-out process may be more severe; therefore, clinicians must be judicious when encouraging multiethnic/multiracial consumers to come out.

CBMCS

Socioeconomic Status (SES)

CBMCS

Socioeconomic Status (SES)

"The right to be free of the crushing burden of poverty must be counted among the most fundamental of human rights. Poverty is brutal. It is embedded in all realms of the existence of poor people, and extends beyond lack of income."

(Speth, 1998, p. 282)

CBMCS

Poverty

- Poverty is a condition in which one is unable to take care of basic needs adequately and consistently (i.e., food, shelter).
- 2004 statistics show that there are 37 million people living in poverty in the U.S., representing 12.7% of the population.
- In California, Imperial, Fresno, and Tulare counties have highest poverty rates (>18%); Marin, San Mateo, and Placer counties show lowest rates (<7.5%).
- Estimated 3.5 million people likely to be homeless in a given year. Almost half are children.

(National Coalition for the Homeless, 2006; U.S. Census Bureau, 2006)

CBMCS

Poverty (continued)

Poverty Rates by Race and Hispanic Origin: 2004

Race and Hispanic Origin	Poverty Rate (percentage)	Percentage Point Change From 2003
White, not Hispanic	8.6	–0.4
Black	24.7	No Change
Asian	9.8	–2.0
Hispanic origin (any race)	21.9	No Change

- 3-year average rates for Alaskan Natives/American Indians was between 20% and 23%

Source: U.S. Census Bureau, Current Population Survey, 2004 and 2005 Annual Social and Economic Supplements.

Poverty (continued)

Poverty Rates by Age: 1959 to 2004

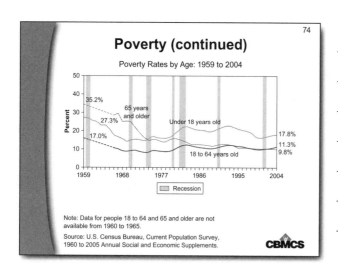

Note: Data for people 18 to 64 and 65 and older are not available from 1960 to 1965.

Source: U.S. Census Bureau, Current Population Survey, 1960 to 2005 Annual Social and Economic Supplements.

Poverty (continued)

- May be attributable to:
  - Increase in single-parent families headed by women
  - New jobs in poorly paid service sector
  - Inadequacy of child support payments following divorce
  - Unavailability of decent, affordable child care
  - Lack of access to unemployment compensation
  - Erosion of governmental economic assistance to low-income families
  - Early phase of immigration, which can result in severe financial struggle
  - Generational poverty

(Dalaker & Proctor, 2000; Hopps & Liu, 2006; Smith, 2005)

Common Myths and Misperceptions About Poverty

- Poor people are lazy.
- People on public assistance are "freeloaders."
- Poor people are mostly minorities.
- Poor people have too many children and have more children to increase their welfare checks.
- Programs to help the poor are draining the budget.
- Most poor people are long-term poor.
- Most poor people are from the inner city.

Health Disparities

Race/ethnicity is disproportionately associated with poverty and health disparities.

- The Institute of Medicine's 2003 book titled *Unequal Treatment* indicates that racial/ethnic minorities experience disproportionate health disparities compared with white populations (Institute of Medicine, 2003).
- Mental health services are plagued by disparities in the availability of and access to its services, and these disparities are viewed readily through the lenses of racial and cultural diversity, age, and gender (U.S. DHHS, 2001).
- A major finding of the U.S. DHHS report is that racial and ethnic minorities bear a greater burden from unmet mental health needs and thus suffer a greater loss to their overall health and productivity (U.S. DHHS, 2001).

(LaVeist, 2005)

The Uninsured Predicament

- The U.S. surgeon general's report reveals that the uninsured predicament in the U.S. may serve as a critical barrier to the access of health care.
- There are 45.8 million uninsured in the U.S.; 8.3 million are children (11.2%).
- The majority of uninsured Americans work (74%), either full-time (46%) or part-time (28%).
- Uninsured Americans come from every race, age, and ethnic group.

(LaViest, 2005; U.S. Department of Health and Human Services, 2005)

Uninsured: Rates by Race

Race and Hispanic Origin	Uninsured Rate (percentage)	Percentage Point Change From 2003
White, not Hispanic	11.3	No Change
Black	19.7	No Change
Asian	16.8	−2.0
Hispanic origin (any race)	32.7	No Change

Source: U.S. Census Bureau, Current Population Survey,
2004 and 2005 Annual Social and Economic Supplements.

Class Distinctions

- Underclass: includes those who have been left behind by contemporary economic developments and who are likely to be unemployed and dependent on public assistance
- Lower class: composed of displaced and poor who have little formal education and are often unemployed or working in minimum-wage jobs
- Lower middle class: includes workers in the skilled trades and low-income bureaucratic workers
- Middle class: mostly white-collar workers
- Upper middle class: those with high income and high social prestige (e.g., well-educated professionals and business executives)
- Nouveau riche: individuals with newly acquired wealth
- Upper class: those who have inherited money at the pinnacle of the class structure

(Andersen & Taylor, 2004)

Mental Illness and Socioeconomic Status

- People from lowest socioeconomic strata are 2 to 3 times more likely to have a mental disorder and higher levels of distress than those in higher strata.
- Poverty increases risk for mental disorders through greater exposure to stressful environments (e.g., violence, unemployment) and less buffering from social or material resources.
- Conversely, having a mental disorder increases risk for poverty through reduced functioning and productivity.
- Poverty and race are intertwined due to legacy of racism and discrimination.
- Even within impoverished environments, there may exist multiple protective factors that increase resilience and limit mental illness.

(Unger, 2005; U.S. Department of Health and Human Services, 2001)

Treatment Considerations

Provider must become aware of the following:

- Attitudes, beliefs, assumptions, values, and bias toward those who do not share one's same socioeconomic status.
- The need to assess consumer's presenting problem thoroughly so as to not misdiagnose or fail to properly define the problem.
- The consumer may hold a different worldview and value system.
- Consumer's failure to show up for services may be attributed to lack of financial resources for transportation, day care, etc.
- Consumers may require additional support and resources in completing paperwork or other mandates due to lack of educational attainment and skill.
- Cognitive-behavioral strategies may be inappropriate if homework assignments are unrealistic because of the consumer's financial situation.

(Smith, 2005)

Treatment Considerations (continued)

- The consumer may have experienced discrimination and oppression due to poverty level.
- The consumer may not have the same access to health care, including medication.
- Consumer may be more at risk of mental health problems due to the interaction of multiple identities (SES, race/ethnicity, age, physical ability, gender, sexual orientation).
- There may exist within-group differences among the poor. Every poor person is not impoverished, and may demonstrate areas of resiliency.

(Smith, 2005)

CBMCS

Persons With Disabilities

CBMCS

Disabilities

"Disability only becomes a tragedy when society fails to provide the things we need to live our lives; job opportunities or barrier free buildings for examples. It is not a tragedy for me that I'm living in a wheelchair."

—Judy Heumann, disability activist and former Assistant Secretary for the Office of Special Education and Rehabilitation Services

CBMCS

Myths

- Most persons with disabilities are in wheelchairs, crutches, or walkers.
- People with physical disabilities also have mental disabilities.
- The greatest barriers to persons with disabilities are physical barriers.
- Government health insurance covers people with disabilities.
- Stereotypes against persons with mobility impairments contribute to the erroneous belief that they are asexual.

CBMCS

Knowledge

According to the 2000 census
- 49.7 million persons (19.3%) reported some type of long-lasting disability. Of this group:
  - 6.3% had a sensory disability (sight, hearing)
  - 8.2% had physical/mobility limitations
- Disability rates by race/ethnicity:
  - 24.3% African American
  - 24.3% American Indian/Native Alaskan
  - 20.9% Hispanic
  - 19% Hawaiian/Pacific Islander
  - 18.3% white, not Hispanic
  - 16.6% Asian

(Waldrup & Stern, 2003; also see Sotnik & Jezewski, 2005, for more information)

CBMCS

Variations

- In addition to the variations in the nature of disabilities, persons with disabilities also vary in terms of age of onset of the disability; severity; the extent to which they identify with their disability status; the degree to which their condition is accepted by others; and the diversity in their age, gender, sexual orientation, ethnicity, and socioeconomic class.

(Lee, 1999)

Americans With Disabilities Act (1990)

- Extended the the federal mandate of nondiscrimination toward individuals with disabilities to state and local governments and the private sector.
- Congress defined disability as "a physical or mental impairment that substantially limits one or more of the major life activities of such individual." Includes individuals with mental retardation, psychiatric disorders, hearing impairment, orthopedic impairments, learning disabilities, speech impairment, and other health or physical impairments.

Ableism

- Persons with disabilities have been subjected to stereotypes and negative perceptions, known as ableism.
- Stereotypes of persons with disabilities portray them as abnormal, helpless, heroic and inspirational, invisible, childlike, in need of pity or charity.

(Murphy & Murphy, 1997)

Three Models of Disability

- Moral model—Disability is a defect caused by a moral lapse or sins, failure of faith, evil, or test of faith.
- Medical model—Disability is due to a defect in or failure of a bodily system that is inherently abnormal and pathological.
- Social model—Disability is a social construct. Problems reside in the environment that fails to accommodate people with disabilities.

(Olkin, 2002)

CBMCS

Hearing Impairment: Statistics

- Approximately 28 million persons in the U.S. have a hearing impairment.
- Older adults experience significant rates of hearing impairment.
- 90% of deaf and hard-of-hearing children have parents who are hearing.
- 46% to 60% of the deaf population deals with unemployment, substance abuse, criminal behavior, or poor mental health.
- Although approximately 40,000 persons with hearing impairment experience poor mental health, only 1 in 50 receive mental health services.

(Lee, 1999)

CBMCS

Hearing Impairment: Language

- Language is an important concern when counseling persons with a disability, particularly among clients with hearing impairments.
- Hearing aids are not always helpful, since they often amplify all noises.
- Only 30% of spoken English is understandable through lip reading, making American Sign Language (ASL) the primary language for full communication. However, not all consumers read lips or are ASL proficient.

(Steinberg et al., 1998)

CBMCS

Slide 94

Hearing Impairment: Deaf Culture

- Deaf persons view themselves as part of a linguistic and cultural minority and not as disabled.
- People who identify with deafness as a minority group experience tend to capitalize the *D* in *Deaf* as an indication of cultural identification, whereas *deaf* with a small *d* refers to the physical condition and is used frequently among persons who lost their hearing as adults.

(Steinberg et al., 1998)

Slide 95

Visual Impairment: Statistics

- According to the 2000 U.S. Census, 937,000 (0.78%) of persons older than 40 years were blind; an additional 2.4 million (1.98%) had low vision.
- Low vision and blindness increase with age; about 17% of persons age 65 and older are blind or severely visually impaired.
- 12.2 per 1,000 individuals under age 18 have visual impairments.
- Great variability among persons with visual impairments because 70% to 80% of all legally blind persons have some sight.
- Causes of blindness vary by race/ethnicity.

(Congdon et al., 2004; National Eye Institute, 2004)

Slide 96

Visual Impairment: Myths About Blindness

- Blind people have a sixth sense or extraordinary talents.
- Blind people live in a world of total darkness.
- Strong enough glasses will help anyone who is visually impaired.
- A guide dog knows how to get its master where he or she wants to go.
- All blind people read Braille.
- You need to speak louder when talking to a blind person.
- Blind people can always identify you by your voice.
- In order to travel independently, a blind person needs a guide dog.

(Web, 2005; also see Braille Institute, 2004)

Visual Impairment: Mental Health and Counseling Issues

- Estimates of alcohol and other drug abuse in the blind and visually impaired range from 35% to 50% (van der Wal, 2002).
- Rehabilitation studies on adjustment to loss of sight suggest that providers can help consumers feel motivated and personally successful during the rehabilitation process. Successful adjustment may prevent depressive symptoms (Dodds & Ferguson, 1994; Travis, Boerner, Reinhardt, & Horowitz, 2004).
- Support groups for adults are successful in renewing self-confidence and promoting emotional camaraderie (Jaffe, 1999).
- Social skills and short-term counseling groups for children and adolescents may enhance self-perception, assertiveness, friendship skills, familial relationships, and independent living skills (Johnson & Johnson, 1991; Mar & Sall, 1995).

CBMCS

Mobility Impairments

- U.S. Census (2000) data show rates of physical disability to be 1% in ages 5 to 15 yrs; 6.2% in ages 16 to 64; and 28.6% in age 65 and older. A large subpopulation of persons with mobility impairments are persons with spinal cord injuries.
- Rates of physical disability are similar in males and females, until 65 yrs and older.
- Age of onset is highest among persons within the 15 to 24 age group.

(Waldrup & Stern, 2003)

CBMCS

Cognitive Disabilities

- Cognitive disabilities include dementias, learning disorders, mental retardation, and disabilities due to brain injury, infection, stroke, or tumor.
- The full impact of cognitive disabilities is unknown because some conditions may be hidden (e.g., learning disability) and may not be included in reported statistics.
- Older adults are more likely than younger adults to experience dementia.

(Harris, 2005)

CBMCS

Cognitive Disabilities (continued)

- Many adults who are now diagnosed with learning disabilities may not have known that they had a disability for years since diagnostic testing may not have been easily available in their youth.
- Children and adolescents with learning disabilities are also at risk for developing low self-esteem or learning styles that affect their productivity.
- Children who are severely emotionally disturbed (SED) are often regarded as possessing an invisible disability and are overlooked.

(Harris, 2005)

Developmental Disabilities

- There are nearly 4 million Americans with developmental disabilities (about 1.58%).
- Developmental disabilities are severe, chronic disabilities attributable to mental and/or physical impairment, which manifest before age 22 and are likely to continue indefinitely.
- They result in substantial limitations in three or more areas—self-care, receptive and expressive language, learning, mobility, self-direction, capacity for independent living, and economic self-sufficiency— as well as the need for individually planned and coordinated services.

(Developmental Disabilities Assistance and Bill of Rights Act of 2000; Lee, 1999)

Cultural Perspectives Regarding Disability

- Cultural values impact how individuals and families deal with disabilities.
- Asian Americans: Disability may be seen as punishment for having sinned and creates shame. Mothers may believe they did something wrong during pregnancy (Stone, 2005).
- Latinos: Disability may be seen as an act of God or as a punishment from God. Concern about economic impact of the disability. Gender role conflicts may occur (Marini, 2001).

Cultural Perspectives
Regarding Disability (continued)

- Some Native Americans do not view disability as a punishment for having sinned and treat their members as they would anyone else (Marini, 2001).
- African Americans often believe that all people are God's children, including persons with disabilities. Support from the church, extended family members, and role flexibility contribute to successful adjustment (Marini, 2001).

Cultural Perspectives
Regarding Disability (continued)

- Issues of disabilities are also complex for LGBT due to health insurance policies, legal wills, other survivor preparations, and AIDS-related discrimination.

(Quitnner, 2004; see also www.lambdalegal.org)

Treatment Considerations

- Providers are seldom trained to work with clients with disabilities.
- Providers need to address their discomfort in working with consumers with disabilities and recognize that they are also subject to disability prejudice.

(Sue & Sue, 2003)

Treatment Considerations
(continued)

- Need to identify personal views of consumers with disabilities and prejudicial assumptions.
- A consumer's disability should not be the sole focus of counseling.
- Environmental contributions to problems should also be examined.
- Issues involving frustration with architectural barriers or negative stereotypes should be examined.

Treatment Considerations
(continued)

- Errors of omission—Failure to ask questions because of the assumption that the issue, such as relationships or sexuality, is unimportant due to the presence of a disability.
- Errors of commission—Assumption that certain issues (e.g., loss of hearing or vision) are important because of a disability when they are not.

Treatment Considerations
(continued)

- Providers need to make sure that their rooms are accessible, plan for unavoidable tardiness due to transportation delays, delays with personal assistants, and accommodate absences caused by required medical treatment.

109

Treatment Considerations
(continued)

- For consumers experiencing psychiatric disabilities, mental health providers must be vigilant to address co-occurring disabilities as appropriate.
- Provide auxiliary aids and services when needed.
- Evaluate your office for structural or architectural barriers.
- Develop self-advocacy skills in consumer and family and recognize advocacy/consulting role played by provider.

110

Specific Treatment Considerations for Consumers With Hearing Impairments

- Become aware of assumptions, biases about deafness, and issues of prejudice and discrimination specific to the deaf population.
- Evaluate provider knowledge and proficiency in counseling deaf persons to see if it matches consumers' needs and preferences. Assist with referral if necessary.
- Learn how to find a qualified ASL interpreter and work with him or her as a team. Face and speak to the consumer, not the interpreter.
- Make sure you have the consumer's attention before speaking. Rephrase sentences rather than repeat them.
- Communicate in writing if necessary, but do not assume that the consumer is literate in written English.

(Williams & Abeles, 2004)

111

Specific Treatment Considerations for Consumers With Visual Impairments

- Ask if any particular assistance is needed.
- Respect companion dogs; do not attempt to pet or play with them.
- Orient the person to the area, explaining where major furniture is located.
- Keep doors fully open or closed to prevent accidents.
- Use of sighted idioms, such as "see you later" are okay and also used by the visually impaired.
- When giving directions, use specific words such as "forward" or "straight ahead."

(Johnson & Johnson, 1991; Web, 2005)

112

Specific Treatment Considerations for Consumers With Mobility Impairments

- Ask if assistance is required.
- Do not remove a person's mobility aid, for example crutches, without the person's consent.
- When talking to someone who is in a wheelchair for more than a few minutes, sit down to be at eye level. This avoids neck strain and is much more positive.
- Do not touch or lean on a person's wheelchair unless you have his or her permission—it is a part of the person's body space.
- Use "person-first" terms such as "person who uses a wheelchair," rather than "disabled person."
- Make sure your facilities are accessible and ADA-compliant— for example, wide and uncluttered aisles, ramps, elevators, curb cuts, and restroom access.

(Waldrup & Stern, 2003)

CBMCS

113

Activity: The Interaction Between Multiple Identities

CBMCS

114

Activity: Identity Map

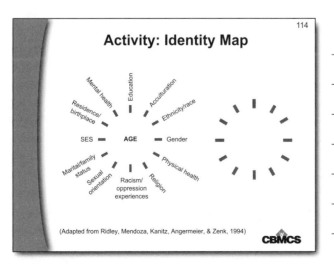

(Adapted from Ridley, Mendoza, Kanitz, Angermeier, & Zenk, 1994)

CBMCS

Conclusion

115

CBMCS

Handouts

Module 4 Handout 1 (Slide 12)

List of Consumer Populations

Please rank order the following diverse consumer populations in terms of your preferences for working with them professionally in a mental health setting (assuming, of course, that you possessed the requisite skills for making contact and there were collateral mental health problems in addition). Begin with 1 for the population you are most favorably disposed toward to work with as a provider. Try to avoid ties.

_____ Adolescent	_____ Indigent man
_____ Adults	_____ Indigent woman
_____ Adult man	_____ Mentally challenged child
_____ Adult woman	_____ Mentally challenged man
_____ Senior man	_____ Mentally challenged woman
_____ Senior woman	_____ Physically impaired man
_____ Visually impaired man	_____ Physically impaired woman
_____ Visually impaired woman	_____ Cognitively impaired man
_____ Children	_____ Cognitively impaired woman
_____ Hearing-impaired man	_____ Man with schizophrenia
_____ Hearing-impaired woman	_____ Woman with schizophrenia
_____ Gay man	_____ Speech-impaired man
_____ Lesbian woman	_____ Speech-impaired woman

List 1, 2, 3 consumer ranks:
1. _____
2. _____
3. _____
List 24, 25, 26 consumer ranks:
24. _____
25. _____
26. _____
List your number for man with schizophrenia: _____
List your number for woman with schizophrenia: _____

Module 4 Handout 2 (Slide 114)

Vignette A: Sexual Orientation/Social Class/Ethnicity

The consumer is a 19-year-old bisexual Asian American man, born of Cambodian immigrant parents who are currently unemployed white-collar professionals. The consumer dropped out of high school in his senior year and is fully acculturated. He is currently looking for work and lives at home with his parents. He presents with anxiety, anger, and depression concerning his inability to explain his sexual identity to his non-English-speaking parents. He is also experiencing perceived racial discrimination in his job search.

Module 4 Handout 2 (Slide 114)

Vignette B: Age/Disability/Gender/Social Class/Race

The consumer is a 70-year-old African American woman, confined to a wheelchair for 10 years after a serious car accident. She is a lifelong smoker and has been diagnosed with emphysema. She lives with her 20-year-old granddaughter on welfare and her unemployed boyfriend in an industrial part of town. Two young children also live with them. Her mental status exam clearly shows that she is clinically depressed, with a history of substance abuse. She reports being a burden to those around her and expresses the desire to end her life.

Module 4 Handout 2 (Slide 114)

Generic Identity Map

SOURCE: Adapted from Ridley, Mendoza, Kanitz, Angermeier, and Zenk (1994).

References

Alderson, K. G. (2003). The ecological model of gay male identity. *Canadian Journal of Human Sexuality, 12,* 75–85.

American Psychological Association. (1998a, July). Answers to your questions about sexual orientation and homosexuality-revised version. *APA Public Interest.* Washington, DC: Author. Retrieved November 15, 2007, from www.apa.org/topics/orientation.html

American Psychological Association. (1998b). *Guidelines for psychotherapy with lesbian, gay, and bisexual clients.* Washington, DC: Author. (Available at www.apa.org/pi/lgbc/publications/guidelines.html)

American Psychological Association. (2005, April). *Aging Issues: E-Newsletter of the APA Office on Aging, 3*(1).

Andersen, M. L., & Taylor, H. F. (2004). *Sociology: Understanding a diverse society.* New York: Wadsworth.

Braithwaite, V. (2002). Reducing ageism. In T. D. Nelson (Ed.). *Ageism: Stereotyping and prejudice against older persons* (pp. 311–337). Cambridge: MIT Press.

Butler, R. N. (1969). Age-ism: Another form of bigotry. *The Gerontologist, 9,* 243.

Butler, R. N. (2002). *Why survive? Being old in America.* Baltimore, MD: John Hopkins University Press.

California Mental Health Planning Council. (2003, March). *California mental health master plan: A vision for California.* Retrieved May 31, 2007, from www.dmh.cahwnet.gov/MHPC/docs/Master%20Plan/mstrplan.pdf

Canales, G. (2000). Gender as subculture: The first division of multicultural diversity. In I. Cuéllar & F. A. Paniagua (Eds.), *Handbook of multicultural mental health: Assessment and treatment of diverse populations* (pp. 63–77). San Diego, CA: Academic Press.

Cass, V. C. (1979). Homosexual identity formation: A theoretical model. *Journal of Homosexuality, 4,* 219–235.

Coleman, E. (1982). Developmental stages of the coming-out process. *American Behavioral Scientist, 25,* 469–482.

Congdon, N., O'Colmain, B., Klaver, C. C., Klein, R., Munoz, B., Friedman, D. S., et al. (2004). Causes and prevalence of visual impairment among adults in the United States. *Archives of Ophthalmology, 122,* 477–485.

Connors, P. G. (Ed.). (2008). *Homosexuality.* Detroit, MI: Greenhaven Press.

Cox, C. B. (2005). Ethnicity and care. In *Community care for an aging society: Issues, policies, and services* (pp. 134–152). New York: Springer.

Dalaker, J., & Proctor, B. D. (2000). Poverty in the United States: 1999. U.S. Census Bureau, *Current Populations Reports, Series P,* 60–210. Washington, DC: Government Printing Office.

Developmental Disabilities Assistance and Bill of Rights Act of 2000, PL 106-402, 114 Stat. 1677 (2000). Retrieved November 15, 2007, from www.acf.hhs.gov/programs/add/ddact/DDACT2.html

Dodds, A., & Ferguson, E. (1994). The concept of adjustment: A structural model. *Journal of Visual Impairment & Blindness, 88,* 487.

Dworkin, S. H., & Gutierrez, F. (1989). Introduction to special issue. Counselors be aware: Clients come in every size, shape, color, and sexual orientation. *Journal of Counseling and Development, 68,* 6–8.

Gatz, M., & Pearson, C. G. (1988). Ageism revised and the provision of psychological services. *American Psychologist, 43,* 184–188.

Greene, B. (2005). Psychology, diversity and social justice: Beyond heterosexism and across the cultural divide. *Counseling Psychology Quarterly, 18,* 295–306.

Harris, J. C. (2005). *Intellectual disability.* New York: Oxford University Press.

Herek, G. M. (2004). Beyond "homophobia": Thinking about sexual stigma and prejudice in the twenty-first century. *Sexuality Research and Social Policy, 1,* 6–24.

Hill, R. D., Thorn, B. L., & Packard, T. (2000). Counseling older adults: Theoretical and empirical issues in prevention and intervention. In S. D. Brown & R. W. Lent (Eds.), *Handbook of counseling psychology* (3rd ed., pp. 499–531). New York: John Wiley.

Hinrichsen, G. A. (2006). Why multicultural issues matter for practitioners working with older adults. *Professional Psychology: Research & Practice, 33,* 337–340.

Hopps, J. A., & Liu, W. M. (2006). Working for social justice from within the health system: The role of social class in psychology. In R. L. Toporek, L. H. Gerstein, N. A. Fouad, G. Roysircar, & T. Israel (Eds.), *Handbook for social justice in counseling psychology: Leadership, vision, and action* (pp. 318–337). Thousand Oaks, CA: Sage.

Institute of Medicine. (2003). *Unequal treatment: Confronting racial and ethnic disparities of health care.* Washington, DC: National Academics Press.

Internet Modern History Sourcebook. (1997). *Sojourner Truth: "Ain't I a Woman."* Retrieved May 31, 2007, from www.fordham.edu/Halsal/mod/somtruth-woman.html

Israel, T. (2003). Integrating gender and sexual orientation into multicultural counseling. In G. Roysircar, P. Arredondo, J. N. Fuertes, J. G. Ponterotto, & R. L. Toporek (Eds.), *Multicultural counseling competencies 2003: Association for multicultural counseling and development* (pp. 69–77). Alexandria, VA: American Counseling Association.

Jaffe, M. S. (1999). Support group for adults with cortical visual impairment: An innovative model. *Journal of Visual Impairment & Blindness, 93,* 728–733.

Janus, S. S., & Janus, C. L. (1993). *The Janus report: Sexual behavior.* New York: John Wiley.

Jenny, C., & Roesler, T. A. (1994). Are children at risk for sexual abuse by homosexuals? *Pediatrics, 94,* 41–44.

Johnson, C. L., & Johnson, J. (1991). Using short-term group counseling with visually impaired adolescents. *Journal of Visual Impairment & Blindness, 85,* 166–170.

LaVeist, T. A. (2005). *Minority populations and health: An introduction to health disparities in the United States.* San Francisco: Jossey-Bass.

Lee, R. M., & Dean, B. L. (2004). Middle-class mythology in an age of immigration and segmented assimilation: Implication for counseling psychology. *Journal of Counseling Psychology, 51,* 10–24.

Lee, W. M. (1999). *An introduction to multicultural counseling.* Philadelphia: Accelerated Development.

Mar, H. H., & Sall, N. (1995). Enhancing social opportunities and relationships of children who are deaf-blind. *Journal of Visual Impairment & Blindness, 89*(3), 280–286.

Marini, I. (2001). Cross-cultural counseling issues of males who sustain a disability. *Journal of Applied Rehabilitation Counseling, 32,* 36–44.

National Coalition for the Homeless. (2006). *Hate, violence, and death on main street USA: A report on hate crimes and violence against people experiencing homelessness, 2006.* Retrieved by June 1, 2007, from www.nationalhomeless.org/publications/reports.html

National Eye Institute. (2004). *Statistics and data.* Retrieved June 1, 2007, from www.nei.nih.gov/eyedata

Nelson, T. B. (Ed.). (2002). *Ageism: Stereotyping and prejudice against older persons.* Cambridge: MIT Press.

Olkin, R. (2002). Could you hold the door for me? Including disability in diversity. *Cultural Diversity and Ethnic Minority Psychology, 8,* 130–137.

Olson, L. K. (2001). *Age through ethnic lenses: Caring for the elderly in a multicultural society.* Lanham, MD: Rowman & Littlefield.

Pharr, S. (1988). *Homophobia: A weapon of sexism.* Little Rock, AR: Chardon Press.

Sax, L. (2002). How common is intersex? A response to Anne Fausto-Sterling. *Journal of Sex Research, 39,* 174–179.

Smith, L. B. (2005). Psychotherapy, classism, and the poor: Conspicuous by their absence. *American Psychologist, 60,* 687–696.

Sotnik, P., & Jezewski, M. A. (2005). Culture and disability services. In J. H. Stone (Ed.), *Culture and disability* (pp. 15–36). Thousand Oaks, CA: Sage.

Speth, J. G. (1998). Poverty: A denial of human rights. *Journal of International Affairs, 52,* 277–293.

Sue, S., & Sue, D. W. (2000). Conducting psychological research with the Asian American/Pacific Islander population. In Council of National Psychological Associations for the Advancement of Ethnic Minority Interests (Ed.), *Guidelines for research in ethnic minority communities* (pp. 2–4). Washington, DC: American Psychological Association.

Travis, L. A., Boerner, K., Reinhardt, J. P., & Horowitz, A. (2004). Exploring functional disability in older adults with low vision. *Journal of Vision Impairment & Blindness, 98,* 534–545.

Unger, M. (Ed.). (2005). *Handbook for working with children and youth: Pathways to resilience across cultures and contacts.* Thousand Oaks, CA: Sage.

U.S. Census Bureau. (2000). *Census 2000 demographic data products.* Retrieved November 19, 2007, from www.census.gov/population/www/censusdata/c2k_subs.html

U.S. Census Bureau. (2005). *News conference on 2004 income, poverty, and health insurance estimates from the current population survey* [Press briefing]. Retrieved November 11, 2007, from www. census.gov/hhes/www/income/income04/prs05asc.html

U.S. Census Bureau. (2006, August 24). *International data base (IDB).* Retrieved May 30, 2007, from http://www.census.gov/ipc/www/idnew.html

U.S. Department of Health and Human Services. (1999). *Mental health: A report of the surgeon general.* Rockville, MD: Author.

U.S. Department of Health and Human Services. (2001). *Mental health: Culture, race, and ethnicity: A supplement to mental health: A report of the surgeon general—Executive summary.* Rockville, MD: Author.

van der Wal, A. (2002). Alcohol abuse and blindness. *Blindwork Association Insight Newsletter, 27*(3), Retrieved November 19, 2007, from http://avreus.org/Summer%202002.htm

Waldrup, J., & Stern, S. M. (2003). *Disability status 2000: A census 2000 brief.* Washington, DC: U.S. Census Bureau, U.S. Department of Commerce, Economics and Statistics Administration. Retrieved November 19, 2007 from www.census.gov/prod/2003pubs/c2kbr-17.pdf

Westheimer, R. K., & Lopater, S. (2005). *Human sexuality: A psychosocial perspective* (2nd ed.). Baltimore, MD: Lippincott, Williams, & Wilkins.

Williams, C., & Abeles, N. (2004). Issues and implications of deaf culture in therapy. *Professional Psychology: Research and Practice, 35,* 643–648.